Between Work & Leisure

Between Work & Leisure

The Common Ground of Two Separate Worlds

Robert A. Stebbins

Transaction Publishers
New Brunswick (U.S.A.) and London (U.K.)

Library of Congress Catalog Number: 2004041281
ISBN: 0-7658-0227-9
Printed in the United States of America

Library of Congress Cataloging-in-Publication Data

Stebbins, Robert A., 1938-
    Between work and leisure : the common ground of two separate worlds
/ Robert A. Stebbins.
        p. cm.
    Includes bibliographical references and index.
    ISBN 0-7658-0227-9 (alk. paper)
    1. Leisure. 2. Work. 3. Voluntarism. I. Title.

HD4904.6.S7   2004
306.3'6—dc22   2004041281

To Jack and Jackie Lindstrom,
two occupational devotees

Work thou for pleasure – paint, or
sing, or carve
The thing thou lovest, though the body
starve —
Who works for glory misses oft the
Goal;
Who works for money coins his very
soul.
Work for the work's sake, then, and it
may be
That these things shall be added unto
thee.

Kenyon Cox. *The gospel of art* (1895)

Contents

Preface

This book explores the social, cultural, and social psychological conditions that have drawn and will likely continue to draw occupational devotees to their work, captivated as they are by the many profound and exceptional cultural values and intrinsic rewards they realize there. Neither the psychology of occupations nor the sociology of work has shed much light on the conditions or the devotees. A main reason for this neglect is that both fields have failed to recognize the common ground they share with their counterparts in leisure research, the study of a world where some people pursue with great enthusiasm the same activities that occupational devotees enthusiastically pursue at work. I argue in this book that much can be learned about devotee work from research done on its leisure equivalent. The knowledge gained from this endeavor should be welcome for, as Richard Florida (2002, p. 88) has observed, little hard quantitative research or analysis exists on the motivation of what he calls the "creative worker."

Occupational devotion is a strong and positive attachment to a form of self-enhancing work, where the sense of achievement is high and the core activity (set of tasks) is endowed with such intense appeal that the line between this work and leisure is virtually erased. This devotion is evident in the actions, lifestyle, and social relations of the *occupational devotee.* In working at the core activity, it is argued here, devotees realize a unique combination of strongly seated cultural values: success, achievement, freedom of action, individual personality, and activity in the form of work. Others categories of workers may also be animated by some or all of these values, but fail for various reasons to realize them through employment.

Indeed, the blunt truth is that most people work out of necessity, not out of profound love for the job and a set of deeply felt values that they realize there. Granted, some of these people derive certain agreeable, albeit comparatively superficial, rewards from the work they must do to support themselves, including its social life, the positive recognition that comes with being employed (as opposed to unemployed), and the fact that working helps time pass. But none of this is nearly as appealing as finding deep fulfillment in the central activities that constitute the occupation, which is what distinguishes the occupational devotee. Moreover, others who work out of necessity may even fail to find superficial rewards in their jobs, the regular paycheck being the only substantial reason for staying with them.

But neither the dislike of work nor the superficial rewards it sometimes offers are the concern of this book. Nor should they be, for the reality is that, to quote Eliot Freidson (1990, p. 149), "most of what has been written about work through the ages is hostile in character." What is needed now, and what is undertaken here, is an examination of the "friendly" side of work: what is it about some kinds of work that keeps its devotees enthusiastically returning for more?

Regarding intrinsically attractive work, which is so very much like certain forms of leisure, many of the aforementioned social, psychological, and social psychological conditions have actually been discovered through research conducted in the sociology and psychology of leisure. Perhaps it is this curious division of scientific labor that explains why most of these conditions have failed to this day to find a place in contemporary theories of work and occupations. At any rate, I have been studying occupations on and off since my graduate school days in the early 1960s, when I wrote two theses on professional jazz and commercial musicians. Now comes this book, which for me, represents a substantial return to the sociology of work, after having become rather one-sidedly involved with leisure research through a study of amateurs launched late in 1973. I have since that time studied, using exclusively exploratory methodology, eight amateur and five hobbyist pursuits as well as one volunteer field. And there is more to come in all three types. I pioneered the concepts of serious and casual leisure, among several others to have emerged inductively from these investigations. Finally, this is no longer the one-man show it was in the 1970s and early 1980s. Many other scholars, based in North America and elsewhere, are now at work in this area (for a partial summary, see Stebbins, 2001a, chap. 8).

My aim in this book, then, is to lay to rest the prevailing myth (extant in both science and commonsense) that work and leisure are wholly separate and, as often as not, mutually antagonistic spheres of life. The close relationship, set out in detail in this book, between serious leisure and occupational devotion demonstrates that there can be joy in work just as there is in leisure and that the joy felt is, at bottom, qualitatively the same in both worlds. In other words this joy is basically a shared sentiment, in that the core activities in work and leisure which are so powerfully attractive—and which foster the joy—are highly similar, and in some instances, literally identical.

The immediate theoretical framework for this book is the serious/ casual leisure perspective and the emergent framework of occupational devotion, whose rudiments are set out in chapter 1. And, since both have a certain psychological and social psychological slant about them, they need to be placed as well in larger social, cultural, and historical context. Much of this contextualization is accomplished in chapters 2 and 3.

Chapter 1 opens with a discussion of occupational devotion and occupational devotees and then moves on to examine the kinds of work in which devotees are found, their commitment to it, and the values they strive to realize there. Chapter 2 centers on Weber's celebrated treatise on the Protestant ethic, which is, among other things, about becoming motivated to find and succeed in an occupation whose culture emphasizes accumulating capitalist wealth. Motivation generated by the Protestant ethic is essentially extrinsic, however: to be rewarded with eternal salvation for having amassed on earth noteworthy riches. Thus there were always occupations lying outside the purview of Weber's little essay, including those requiring altruistic service to humankind and extensive development of personal skills and knowledge. It is quite possible therefore that, at the time when the Protestant ethic was a prominent motive in the work world, some workers were enamored instead of occupations with great intrinsic appeal.

In any case, the Protestant ethic, as a motive to work, is largely a dead letter today, even while some people still work long hours pursuing a variety of worldly rewards. David Riesman and colleagues (1961) argued that the inner-directed men of the 1950s, who *were* oriented by the Protestant ethic, were being rapidly replaced by other-directed men, whose love of mass culture was a distinguishing feature. Otherworldly as it was, the Protestant ethic, it appears, was nevertheless an important cultural precursor of the modern work ethic. It helped establish the value of work; work is good and hard work is even better.

Later Marilyn Machlowitz (1980) would pioneer the concept of "workaholism," in an attempt to help explain why a conspicuous minority of modern workers, though not guided by the Protestant ethic, are still exceptionally drawn to their work, in part, because of its many intrinsic rewards. Yet, she also defined them as "work junkies," as unfortunates lamentably addicted to their work. These people find joy and fulfillment in their work roles, from which they seem unable to take any real holiday.

Unfortunately, workaholism, as a term, has through careless lay usage become corrupted and distorted to mean, now even for some scientists (e.g., Killinger, 1997; Fassel, 2000), compulsion to work. In this view compulsive workers, who toil well beyond providing the necessities of life, find little of intrinsic worth in their work, only an irresistible impulse to engage in it. In this book, workaholism will refer only to this meaning. These days most people speak most of the time of workaholics as work addicts, either forgetting or overlooking the fact that occupational devotees also exist. Indeed, some of those they casually label workaholic may well be devotees at heart.

The second chapter frames occupational devotion in four broad social contexts: history, religion, work, and to some extent, leisure, with more to be said in chapter 4 on the last of these. This does not, however, exhaust all the angles from which we can look on this orientation and thereby better understand its fit in the larger society in which it is expressed. Accordingly, four additional angles are considered in chapter 3: gender, family, social class, and social character. Each enables us to see another distinctive side of occupational devotion in comparison with the other orientations toward work.

Chapters 4 and 5 form the heart of this book, describing as they do the extensive common group occupied by serious leisure and devotee work. The serious leisure branch of the sociology and psychology of leisure centers on the enthusiasts who do for nothing what others sometimes do for pay. Here research has uncovered a range of deeply felt motives, none having addictive properties. For whatever else leisure is, it is certainly uncoerced behavior, the very antithesis of such properties. This research suggests that some so-called workaholics are in no way work junkies. Indeed, to escape the pejorative, compulsive connotations of workaholism, only its positive side is treated of in this book, accomplished by inquiring into occupational devotion and its incarnation in the occupational devotee. This nomenclature communicates well the powerful, noncoerced, intrinsic appeal that work holds for these devotees, precisely the same kind of appeal it holds (as leisure) for serious leisure enthusiasts.

We know comparatively little about these devotees, in part because they are relatively uncommon, in part because most people today pan all work (their own included) for its perceived dearth of deep-seated intrinsic rewards. In this faultfinding atmosphere occupational devotees stand out as an atypical category of worker, someone who has managed to erase the line between work and leisure. This best-of-all-possible livelihoods suggests that, for them, the only difference between work and leisure is that they get paid to do what some serious leisure participants do for nothing. In short, both intensely love the same activity, finding there a powerfully attractive career. To expand on the words of T. H. Marshall (1963, p. 151), who by the way confined his observations to professionals, these devotees are paid so they may work, whereas most people work so they may be paid. And it is in the study of professionals where some small headway has been made in describing the rewards occupational devotees find in their work (see Karp, 1989).

The research of Stebbins (1992; 2001a) and others (for a review see Stebbins, 2001a, chap. 8) on the "serious leisure" of amateurs, hobbyists, and career volunteers helps explain why occupational devotees, like these serious leisure enthusiasts, are so strongly attracted to their work. Such explanation proceeds from the observation that all amateurs as well as certain kinds of hobbyists and career volunteers do in their leisure what some other people do for a living. In a sense, then, occupational devotees are paid so that they may play, or in some instances aspire to play, full-time at what their serious leisure counterparts play at part-time (except retirees no longer seeking work in any capacity and people temporarily out of work).

Chapter 6 explores the thorny question of the role among these devotees of monetary payment as livelihood. How important is it? What happens when it becomes a major, if not dominant, value, as has happened, for instance, to many athletes in modern professional sport? In this chapter we also take a look at work and leisure in everyday life, examining in particular the issues of selfishness of devotees, devotee leisure lifestyles, and uncontrollability of the activity itself.

Seeing devotee work and serious leisure as compatible occupants of a common terrain rather than as estranged inhabitants living in two separate worlds has numerous implications for society and the individual. Several of these are considered in the final chapter. Well being at work and leisure is addressed as is the question of alienation and bureaucracy. The Information Age forms the context for these discussions and for the proposition that serious leisure can be a substitute for work, even for the devotee. Most central, however, is the section on the relationship between work and leisure, where the common ground shared by these two separate worlds is considered in light of the preceding chapters. Here I introduce the metaphor of work and leisure as constituting two sides of a single coin, intended as counterweight to the prevailing idea that they always occupy separate, sometimes hostile, worlds. The book ends with a lesson on the need to approach the study of occupational devotion using the methodology of exploratory research. The aim has been throughout to set out a framework of concepts capable of guiding open-ended research in his area. The central problem to be explored, then, is the motivation of occupational devotees and how theory and research in serious leisure can help explain it.

This book diverges from other works in the sociology and psychology of work and leisure, in that it centers on what irresistibly draws people to profoundly attractive core work and leisure tasks and decidedly not on what employers try to do to persuade people to work at tasks that are profoundly unattractive. Many of today's work tasks fall in this second category. And since they must be done, employers are forever scrambling to find effective incentives. Much of the literature on work motivation revolves around this problem. But it is also lamentably true that many unattractive jobs can never be made attractive, however thickly we sugarcoat the pill for those working at them. Moreover, some people will have no choice but to work there, while others, if sufficiently aware of their options and qualifications for devotee work, will be able to escape. This book is also written for this second group.

Acknowledgements

I wish to thank Bernard Phillips for encouraging me to undertake this writing project and coaching me in use of the Web approach for framing my ideas. Both Phillips and Irving Louis Horowitz read advanced drafts of the manuscript, with each suggesting a variety of important changes. This advice is deeply appreciated. Laurence Mintz worked assiduously and effectively on copy editing the text; I am most grateful for his efforts in this regard.

1

Occupational Devotion and Occupational Devotees

Kenyon Cox counseled in the epigraph that we should work for pleasure. Good advice. But in this book, in the interest in using the *mot juste*, the object of work will be to find "fulfillment" in pursuing the thing "thou lovest." Pleasure and its twin, enjoyment, describe life's positive but nevertheless superficial experiences, whereas fulfillment most accurately represents our much more deeply felt involvements, the subject of this book.

High fulfillment, though comparatively rare in today's world of work, is nonetheless available in a wide range of occupations, as the following three cases help illustrate.

Charlie Murray Bates—Stonemason

Every piece of stone you pick up is different, the grain's a little different and this and that. It'll split one way and break the other. You pick up your stone and look at it and make an educated guess. It's a pretty good day layin' stone or brick. Not tiring. Anything you like to do isn't tiresome. It's hard work; stone is heavy. At the same time, you get interested in what you're doing and you usually fight the clock the other way. You're not looking for quittin' time. You're wondering you haven't got enough done and it's almost quittin' time.. . .

Stone's my life. I daydream all the time, most time it's on stone. Oh, I'm gonna build me a stone cabin down on the Green River. I'm gonna build stone cabinets in the kitchen. . . . All my dreams, it seems like it's got to have a piece of rock mixed in it. . . .

I can't imagine a job where you go home and maybe go by a year later and you don't know what you've done. My work, I can see what I did the first day I started. All my work is set right out there in the open and I can look at it as I go by. It's something I can see the rest of my life. (Terkel, 1972, pp. xlvi-xlix)

Sarah Houghton—Private School Librarian

On this job, you can *use* your mind. Things that are challenging. Find out what some of the new math phrases mean. Selecting books is a complicated matter. If you have

1

thousands and thousands of dollars in your budget, it doesn't make that much difference if you make a few mistakes. But we're limited here. I must be very frugal.

It's one big room. We're bursting now. Last week we had fifty-eight kids there and there are only seats for fifty-seven. It's a tribute that they like to come there. It's an agonizing night, though, when you have to go around shushing. . . .

I feel free as a bird. I'm in a unique position because I'm the boss. I buy what I like. I initiate things. I can experiment with all kinds of things I think the kids might be interested in. Nobody interferes. For me, it's not chore to go to work. I'm fortunate. Most people never get to do this at any time in their lives. (Terkel, 1972, pp. 542-543)

Bud Freeman-Jazz Musician

I get up at noon. I would only consider myself outside the norm because of the way other people live. They're constantly reminding me I'm abnormal. I could never bear to live the dull lives that most people live, locked up in offices. I live in absolute freedom. I do what I do because I want to do it. What's wrong with making a living doing something interesting?

I wouldn't work for anybody. I'm working for me. . . .

I knew when I was eight years old that I wasn't going to amount to anything in the business world. . . . I wanted my life to have something to do with adventure, something unknown, something involved with a free life, something to do with wonder and astonishment. I loved to play—the fact that I could express myself in improvisation, the *unplanned*. . . .

I've come to love my work. It's my way of life. Jazz is a luxurious kind of music. You don't [lay it all day long. You don't play it all night long. The best way to [play it is in concerts. You're on for an hour or two and you give it everything you have, your best. And the audience is sober. And I'm not in a hurry to have the night finish. Playing nightclubs, it was endless . . . .

If you're a creative player, something must happen, and it will. Some sort of magic takes place, yet it isn't magic. (Terkel, 1972, pp. 458-459)

Occupational Devotion

These three workers are motivated by *occupational devotion*, a strong, positive attachment to a form of self-enhancing work, where the sense of achievement is high and the core activity (set of tasks) is endowed with such intense appeal that the line between this work and leisure is virtually erased. This devotion finds its expression in the *occupational devotee*. Further, it is by way of the core activity and its tasks that devotees realize a unique combination of, what are for them, strongly seated cultural values: success, achievement, freedom of action, individual personality, and activity (being involved in something). Other categories of workers may also be animated by some or all of these values, but fail for various reasons to realize them in their gainful employment. These values will be described in greater detail later in this chapter.

Occupational devotees turn up chiefly, though not exclusively, in four areas of the economy, providing their work there is, at most, only lightly bureaucratized: certain small businesses, the skilled trades, the consulting and counseling occupations, and the public- and client-centered professions. Public-centered professions are found in the arts, sports, scientific, and entertainment fields, while those that are client-centered abound in such fields as law, teaching, accounting, and medicine (Stebbins, 1992, p. 22). It is assumed in all this that the work and its core activity to which people become devoted carries with it a respectable personal and social identity within their reference groups, since it would be difficult, if not impossible, to be devoted to work that those groups regarded with scorn. Still, positive identification with the job is not a defining condition of occupational devotion, since such identification can develop for other reasons, including high salary, prestigious employer, and advanced educational qualifications.

Such identification might also develop through pride of workmanship, but it, too, is not a distinctive condition of occupational devotion. True, occupational devotees are highly likely to exhibit this attitude, even if it is not unique to them. Yet, unskilled laborers can also have pride in what they do, only that what they do is much simpler than what devotees are involved in. Fitting perfectly the spirit of the modern work ethic, the janitor, for instance, can keep a building sparkling clean, be most proud of this effort, and bask in the gratitude of the building's tenants who appreciate such service. Nevertheless, the janitor's work fails to meet several of the defining criteria of occupational devotion set out later in this chapter.

Occupational devotion is a special orientation that some people hold toward their livelihood and, more particularly, toward the routine activities constituting its core. In fact, this core of activity is a major value in its own right; this core is the principal attraction of their work. By way of example: Freeman is in seventh heaven playing jazz saxophone at a concert, as Houghton is in running her library and Bates is when laying stone. There is, for them, huge intrinsic appeal in what they do, such that, had they another source of income and some free time (e.g., income from retirement, another job, or independent wealth), they would be inclined do the activity as leisure. Indeed, the world has many amateur jazz saxophonists and people who work with stone as a hobby and work in libraries as volunteers, all of them pursuing their leisure.

We will, as we go along, encounter other devotee occupations evincing the same basic quality: there exists work—that is, a set of core activities — that can be infectiously attractive. In such work the line between it and leisure is effectively erased. But make no bones about it, devotee work is work, not leisure, in the sense that its devotees are coerced by necessity to find remunerative employment of some kind. Whereas leisure, among its many other distinctive qualities, is decidedly noncoercive (Stebbins, 2002b).

Furthermore, the term occupational devotion tends to mask the fact that, for devotees, the positive side of their occupations is so intensely appealing that it overrides the negative side. In other words, no occupation generates undiluted fulfillment. Freeman says he likes to practice his instrument, but many musicians care little for this aspect of their trade. Houghton dislikes "shushing" talkative students in her library, and one gets the impression (from other parts of his vignette not quoted here) that Bates would rather lay stone than brick. In short, into every occupational devotee's life a little rain does occasionally fall, watering down to a degree the pure fulfillment felt there. But these passing showers fail to dampen significantly that person's overall enthusiasm for the core activity. We'll return in chapter 4 to this ratio of costs to rewards in an activity.

But what about work conditions and love for the highly valued core activity? Freeman found playing jazz in nightclubs to be "endless," presumably because of the occasional drunken and noisy patron who pays scant attention to the music. Perhaps Bates likes much less cutting stone on a hot day than on a cool one. Many a university professor retreats to the office at home, in face of seemingly interminable interruptions suffered while trying to write in the one at school. In these examples, people are working in adversity at their passion, which certainly attenuates its appeal, especially when contrasted with its pursuit under ideal or nearly ideal conditions.

Poor working conditions, whether social or physical, can amount to a cost so poignant that it overrides the love for the core activity, thus forcing the worker into another occupation or, if circumstances permit, early retirement. But in true occupational devotion it is the good conditions that prevail on a reasonably regular basis, with the bad ones, though seen as costs, being nevertheless outweighed by the first. In brief, occupational devotion is only possible if working conditions are defined, *on balance*, as favorable.

Note, however, that some people like their work, primarily because they enjoy the people with whom they work, often talking informally with them as they go about the various tasks that constitute their jobs or socialize with them on official breaks. In addition, or alternatively, they may like the clients or customers they meet. For these workers, who are not occupational devotees, it is not the nature of the work itself that draws them to it (that work is uninteresting), but the social life that goes with it. Yet, at bottom, this social life is not work at all, but leisure seized in the interstices of free time found on the job, even while such leisure helps makes palatable the job itself. Indeed, these work ties may extend into the zone of free time well beyond the place of work, as work friends get together during an evening at a restaurant or an afternoon on the golf course.

But it is questionable how many people who are bored with their work tasks though pleased with their work friends or customers would perform that work for no pay, as leisure. Or how many look forward to going to work after the weekend or equivalent period of time off? Or would they recommend their work as a lifelong career for their children? And what about the fourth "litmus test" in use here— erasing the line between work and leisure? It fails, too, because the humdrum, if not downright unpleasantness, of the core job remains, giving it a manifestly atory and chorelike character.

Saying that people like their work because they enjoy its social life, is much the same as saying that people like their work because it pays well or provides great fringe benefits. All such rewards of the job are extrinsic, rewards found outside the core tasks themselves. By contrast, occupational devotion roots in intrinsic rewards, in values realized by carrying out the work tasks themselves. There is no doubt that extrinsic rewards of the sort just described get people to accept jobs and come to work to perform them. And we should be thankful that people can be motivated thus, for there is much work to be done, comparatively little of which is capable of generating occupational devotion.

And this is not to say that occupational devotees gain no extrinsic rewards, only intrinsic ones. Although the second are key, devotees, too, may enjoy their work colleagues and, relatively rarely it appears, even reap a high rate of pay and benefits. This is the best of all worlds, to be sure, but we shall see later that, as far as work is concerned, this Leibnizian state is all too infrequent. In other words, occupational devotion, as a concept, directs attention to the core activities making up a work role, by proceeding from the assumption that, more than anything else, it is those activities that attract people to and hold them in that role. The four criteria just mentioned—erasing the line between work and leisure, yearning to go to work after the weekend, recommending the work to one's children, and being willing to do the work without pay (as leisure)—serve as reasonably accurate and valid measures of occupational devotion.

Psychological Flow

The intensity with which occupational devotees approach their work suggests that they may at times be in psychological flow there. Flow, a form of optimal experience, is possibly the most widely discussed and studied generic intrinsic reward in the psychology of work and leisure. Although many types of work and leisure generate little or no flow for their participants, those that do are found primarily in the devotee occupations and serious leisure. Still, it will be evident that each work and leisure activity capable of producing flow does so in terms unique to it. And it follows that each of these activities must be carefully studied to discover the properties contributing to its distinctive flow experience.

In his theory of optimal experience, Csikszentmihalyi (1990, pp. 3-5, 54) describes and explains the psychological foundation of the many flow activities in work and leisure, as exemplified in chess, dancing, surgery, and rock climbing. Flow is "autotelic" experience, or the sensation that comes with the actual enacting of intrinsically rewarding activity. Over the years Csikszentmihalyi (1990, pp. 49-67) has identified and explored eight components of this experience. It is easy to see how this quality of work, when present, is sufficiently rewarding and, it follows, highly valued to endow it with many of the qualities of serious leisure, thereby rendering the two inseparable in several ways. And this even though most people tend to think of work and leisure as vastly different. The eight components are

1. sense of competence in executing the activity;

2. requirement of concentration;

3. clarity of goals of the activity;

4. immediate feedback from the activity;

5. sense of deep, focused involvement in the activity;

6. sense of control in completing the activity;

7. loss of self-consciousness during the activity;

8. sense of time is truncated during the activity.

These components are self-evident, except possibly for the first and the sixth. With reference to the first, flow fails to develop when the activity is either too easy or too difficult; to experience flow the participant must feel capable of performing a moderately challenging activity. The sixth component refers to the perceived degree of control the participant has over his or her execution of the activity. This is not a matter of personal competence; rather it is one of degree of influence of uncontrollable external forces, a condition well illustrated in the situation faced by an amateur actress who fretted over the possible behavior of a dog she had to carry around with her during one scene of a play (Stebbins, 1979, p. 107).

Several components of flow as well as its activity-specific nature are evident in the following extracts from Allison and Duncan's (1988, pp. 124-126) study of women who experience it at work.

Most of what I do is economic theory, a lot of problem solving, and I would say that when I'm just sitting at my desk, trying to solve a problem, sometimes I forget about the time, sometimes I have to set an alarm if I'm going to class because I'll forget what time it is.

Developing curriculum and seeing it successful. Motivating faculty. Having the budget come out right, which I work on all the time . . . recruiting people who work out well. Seeing the success in the department that I'm very closely responsible for. Initiating and carrying through is very satisfying.

Yes [I experience this], even in my everyday activities. When we're working on a show. And it would be working with a student who is excited about what he's doing. And also working on my own, a project of my own within the shop. Sometimes I take some of my more difficult costumes and work on them myself, anything that involves tailoring, which is one of my main loves. I can get very involved in that and I find it interesting.

By no means all devotee occupations are capable of generating significant flow, but those that are can be found in all four devotee areas, in the liberal professions (e.g., sport, performing arts, creative writing), in their extensions as consulting or counseling, in certain trades (e.g., stonework, finish carpentry), and in certain small businesses (e.g., custom work, artistic crafts, restoration and repair).

Devotee Occupations

Given how little research there is on the deeply appealing qualities of the enormous variety of occupations found in Western society, it is impossible to present here a detailed statement about these qualities. Freidson (1990) reviews the meager literature on "unalienated" work, in which it is evident that the few observers who have looked into what I am referring to as occupational devotion have failed to tackle the question head on. Indeed, he concludes that "most of what has been written about work through the ages is hostile in character" (Freidson, 1990, p. 149). This observation notwithstanding there is an enormous scientific literature on job satisfaction, where satisfaction is conceptualized much more broadly than occupational devotion as, simply, the degree to which people like their work (Smith, Kendall, and Hullin, 1969). Yet, most people who say they are satisfied with their jobs (and many are not) find only pleasure or contentment in them, which is a far cry from finding profound fulfillment there. To gain a sense of what occupational devotion looks like in real life, then, it must suffice to look at the types of occupations where it is known, or appears likely, to occur.

Before examining these types, let us note, more generally, that, although certain occupations and types of occupations lend themselves much more than others to the generation of devotees, all so-called "devotee occupations" have many workers who cannot be classified thus. These "nondevotees" are, however, significantly less common in the devotee occupations than elsewhere. Nonetheless, for reasons not systematically taken up in this book, the nondevotees have failed to catch the spirit that animates their devotee colleagues. Like the workers mentioned earlier they, too, are motivated largely, if not exclusively, by extrinsic rewards.

I use six criteria to identify devotee occupations. To generate occupational devotion:

1.   the valued core activity must be profound; to perform it acceptability requires substantial skill, knowledge, or experience or a combination of two or three of these;

2.   the core must offer significant variety;

3.   the core must also offer significant opportunity for creative or innovative work, as a valued expression of individual personality. The adjectives "creative" and "innovative" stress that the undertaking results in something new or different, showing imagination and application of routine skill or knowledge. That is, boredom is likely to develop only after the onset of fatigue experienced from long hours on the job, a point at which significant creativity and innovation are no longer possible;

4.   the would-be devotee must have reasonable control over the amount and disposition of time put into the occupation (the value of freedom of action), such that he can prevent it from becoming a burden. Medium and large bureaucracies have tended to subvert this criterion. For, in interest of the survival and development of their organization, managers have felt they must deny their nonunionized employees this freedom, and force them to accept stiff deadlines and heavy workloads. But no activity, be it leisure or work, is so appealing that it invites unlimited participation during waking hours (see chap. 5);

5.   the would-be devotee must have both an aptitude and a taste for the work in question. This is, in part, a case of one man's meat being another man's poison. John finds great fulfillment in being a physician, an occupation that holds little appeal for Jane who, instead, adores being a lawyer (work John finds unappealing); and

6.   the devotees must work in a physical and social milieu that encourages them to pursue often and without significant constraint the core activity. This includes avoidance of excessive paperwork (for an example in medicine, see the *Economist*, 2002, p. 33), caseloads, class sizes, market demands, and the like.

Sounds ideal, if not idealistic, but in fact occupations exist that meet these criteria. We will see later how these criteria also characterize serious leisure, giving further substance to the claim being explored here that it and devotee work occupy a great deal of common ground.

Liberal Professionals

The liberal professions constitute one set of occupations where occupational devotion is noticeably and famously high. These professionals have long been known for the special orientation they hold toward their work. This orientation, which may or may not be shared by the majority of the members of a given profession, reaches its broadest expression in a common outlook that I have referred to as the *spirit of professional work* (Stebbins, 2000). This concept denotes the distinctive set of shared values, attitudes, and expectations that form around a given type of professional work, where as a result of their occupational socialization, the work itself is seen by its practitioners as socially important, highly challenging, intensely absorbing, and for these reasons among others, immensely appealing. This work is highly complicated, executed most effectively by practitioners with many years of training and experience. Additionally, the spirit of professional work pervades the work lives of a sufficient number of employed professionals to constitute an important part of their occupational subculture. Thus, from what is known through research on occupations in general, this spirit, as expressed in each profession, endows the culture of that profession with a special quality not found in any other profession or, more broadly, any other occupation. Karp (1989, p. 751) concludes, after an extensive review of the research literature, that "one of the most consistent research findings in the social science literature is that professionals are relatively more satisfied with their work than nonprofessionals." To expand on the words of T. H. Marshall (1963, p. 151), who by the way confined his observations to professionals, these devotees are paid so they may work, whereas most people work so they may be paid.

But even the professional's work life is not uniformly rosy. Although many professionals find their work meets the six criteria, there is nonetheless a negative side with its costs. So the excitement of professional work stands out in relief against the boring, mundane tasks also required there from time to time (the mundane side of being a judge is discussed by Paterson, 1983, pp. 280-281). Moreover, some professionals, it appears, never escape the ennui of their occupation, a gnawing tension that pushes a significant number of them to leave it at an early or middle stage of their career (Wallace, 1995a). Others, though initially infused with the spirit of professional work, lose it later in their careers and, as a result, seek relief from the boredom in early retirement, a group not to be confused with those professionals who love their work but are forced to retire early for reasons of health or industrial restructuring.

The *Dictionary of Occupational Titles* (U.S. Dept. of Labor Employment and Training Administration, 1991) presents thirteen categories of occupations that qualify as professions using standard sociological definitions of that concept (e.g., Ritzer and Walczak, 1986, p. 62). They are listed below to demonstrate the scope of devotee occupations available at this high level of schooling.

- Occupations in architecture, engineering, and surveying

- Occupations in mathematics and physical sciences

- Computer-related occupations

- Occupations in life sciences

- Occupations in social sciences

- Occupations in medicine and health

- Occupations in education

- Occupations in museum, library, and archival sciences

- Occupations in law and jurisprudence

- Occupations in religion and theology

- Occupations in writing

- Occupations in art

- Occupations in entertainment and recreation

The professions of accounting, social and welfare work, and airline and ship piloting are also listed, but outside these thirteen categories, as are the professions of urban and town planning, graphologist (hand-writing expert), polygraph examiner, and cryptanalyst (expert in secret coding systems).

Many client-centered professionals operate as small businesses, even if some income tax departments may classify them otherwise. The same is true for many public-centered professionals in the fine and entertainment arts. I am speaking here of, at most, lightly bureaucratized enterprises composed of, say, ten employees or less, where the unpleasantness of working in and administrating a complex organization is minimal. The main service of these enterprises and core activity of their entrepreneurs, which is technical advice, is typically provided by people known either as consultants or as counselors.

Consultants and Counselors

The term "consultant" is usually reserved for freelance professionals who are paid for technical advice they give to clients to help the latter solve a problem. Occupational devotion is best observed among full-time consultants, in that part-timers and moonlighters (employees of organizations who consult as a sideline) simply have less time to experience the high fulfillment available in such work. Professional consultants operate in a great range of fields, among them, art, business, careers, and computing as well as nutrition, communications, and human resources. Note, too, that examination of the yellow pages of a typical North American metropolitan telephone book reveals the existence of consulting enterprises that are not, in the sociological sense of the word, professional. If fashion, landscape, and advertising, consultants, for example, are not professionals according to sociological definitions, they are nonetheless freelancers in fields technical enough to be quite capable of generating occupational devotion. Such workers are, however, more accurately classified for the purposes of this book as small businesses.

Such taxonomic confusion does not seem, however, to bedevil the counseling field. Counselors offer technical advice as therapy. Occupational devotion can be most richly observed most among full-time counselors in such professional fields as grief, religion, addictions, and crisis center work as well as family problems, interpersonal relationships, and stress at work. Most counselors are trained as nurses, clergy, psychologists, or social workers.

The yellow pages also contain the occasional reference to "advisers." It appears that some counselors and consultants prefer, whatever the reason, to call themselves advisers. Still, as near as I can tell, there is no distinctive form of work known as advising, even if some occupations include advising in their job descriptions, as seen in the role of university professor that includes advising students on educational and occupational matters.

Skilled Trades

The skilled trades offer the main arena for occupational devotion among blue-collar workers, even though it may also be found among certain kinds of technicians and mechanics. The trades have often been likened by social scientists to the professions, although this "profession-craft model" has been challenged for its lack of empirical support (Silver, 1982, p. 251) and, even as an analogy, it has been shown to have definite limits (Hall, 1986, p. 68). Nonetheless, pride of workmanship, ownership of one's tools, autonomy of working from a blueprint, and skill and fulfillment in use of tools help establish the basis for occupational devotion, the outlet for which is the construction industry. Today automation and deskilling (Braverman, 1974) of blue-collar work have taken their toll, so that "intrinsically gratifying blue-collar jobs are the exception rather than the rule, and are found mainly among the skilled trades" (Rinehart, 1966, p. 131). That some of the trades have hobbyist equivalents in, for instance, wood and metal work, further attests the intrinsic appeal of these activities. Finally, fulfillment in this kind of work appears to be greatest at the top end of the apprentice-journeyman-master scale of experience and licensing.

Small Business Proprietors

The aforementioned consultants and counselors, operating as small businesses, are obvious examples of occupational devotion in this area. But what about other types of small businesses, where occupational devotion is also reasonably common? We can only speculate, since data are scarce. But consider the small *haute cuisine* restaurant open five days a week serving up meals to, say, a maximum of thirty diners, and which thereby provides a manageable outlet for a talented chef. Or the two- or three-person website design service. Or two women who, given their love for working with children, establish a small day-care service. Still, this is a difficult area in which to study occupational devotion, for there are also many small entrepreneurs who feel very much enslaved by their work. The differences here separating devotees from nondevotees revolve primarily around seven criteria, perhaps more: efficiency of the work team and the six criteria of occupational devotion described earlier (skill/ knowledge/ experience; variety; creativity/innovativeness; control; aptitude/taste; social/physical milieu).

Perusal of the yellow pages turned up a fair variety of devotee occupations pursued as small businesses, occupations I then placed in one of eleven categories. This typology should be taken as provisional rather than definitive. For at this, the exploratory stage in the study of occupational devotion, we should expect it to be modified in various ways as suggested by future open-ended research.

The *skilled crafts* are also capable of generating devotee small businesses. Applying the six defining criteria, the work of the handyman, people who remodel homes (internally or externally), and the stonemason serve as three examples. The handyman and those who remodel homes encounter with each project they take on some novelty and some need to be innovative, as does Bates the stonemason.

Teaching as a small business is distinct from professional teaching in primary and secondary schools and institutions of higher education. It is also different from teaching the occasional adult or continuing education course, something usually done as a sideline. Rather teaching as a small business centers on instruction of a practical kind, the demand for which is sufficient to constitute a livelihood for an instructor or small group of instructors. Thus small businesses have been established to teach people how to ride horses, fly small airplanes, and descend to earth in a parachute. Many local dance studios fall into this category, as do driver training schools. Innovativeness here revolves around adapting lessons to the needs of individual students and their capacities to learn the material of the course.

Custom work is another type of small business where occupational devotion abounds. Indeed, compared with other small business fields, it may offer the most fertile soil for this kind of personal growth. Here, to meet the wants of individual customers, the devotee designs (in collaboration with the customer) and sometimes constructs distinctive and personalized new products. Examples include workers who make their living designing and assembling on order special floral arrangements (e.g., bouquets, centerpieces) or gift baskets or confecting such as items as specialty cakes, cookies, or chocolates. Tailors, tatooists, hair stylists, makeup artists, and furniture makers, when working to the specifications of individual customers, also belong in this category. Alternatively, individual customers may be seeking a reshaping or remodeling of something they already possess, such as custom modifications to a car or truck or an item of clothing.

Animal work, though less prevalent than custom work and possibly even less so than devotee handicraft, nevertheless sometimes meets the seven criteria of devotee small business. The main examples here, of which I am aware, are the people who make a living training or showing, cats, dogs, or horses. Just how passionately this work can be pursued is seen in Baldwin and Norris's (1999) study of hobbyist dog trainers.

Evidence that *dealers in collectables* can be occupational devotees also comes from the field of leisure studies, where the love for collecting has been well documented (e.g., Olmsted, 1991). Dealers and collectors work with such items as rare coins, books, stamps, paintings, and antiques. Still dealers are not collectors; that is, their collection, if they have one, is not for sale. But even though dealers acquire collectables they hope to sell for extrinsic speculation and profit, they, like pure collectors, also genuinely know and appreciate their many different intrinsic qualities. Thus, when such collectors face the opportunity to sell at significant profit items integral to their collection (again, if they have one), these motives may clash, causing significant personal tension (Stebbins, in press). Here is an example of a work cost quite capable of diluting occupational devotion.

Repair and restoration center on bringing back an item to its original state. Things in need of repair or restoration and, in the course of doing so, capable of engendering occupational devotion include old clocks and antique furniture as well as fine glass, china, and crockery. There is also a business in restoring paintings. This work, which calls for considerable skill, knowledge, and experience, is typically done for individual customers. It offers great variety and opportunity for creativity and innovation.

The *service occupations* cover a huge area, but only a very small number seem to provide a decent chance to become an occupational devotee. One category with this potential can be labeled "research services." Though most research is conducted by professionals, nonprofessionals do dominate in some fields. Exemplifying the latter are commercial genealogists and investigators concerned with such matters as fraud, crime, and civil disputes as well as industrial disputes, marital wrangles, and missing persons.

The accident reconstruction expert also fits in this category. Day care and dating services as well as the small *haute cuisine* restaurant and the small fund-raising enterprise constitute four other services that can generate occupational devotion, as the earlier examples suggest. And here is the classificatory location of such small business, nonprofessional consultants as those in fashion, landscape, advertising, and the emergent field of personal coaching. By and large, however, the service sector is not the place to look for exciting, fulfilling work, in part because the service itself is often banal, even if important, and in part because of the ever present possibility of fractious customer relations.

The *artistic crafts* offer substantial scope for the would-be occupational devotee. Some are highly specialized, like etching and engraving glass, brass, wood, and marble. Others are more general, including ceramics work and making jewelry. Many people in the artistic crafts are hobbyists, who earn little or no money, whereas other people try to derive some sort of living from them. It is the second group, which consists of many part-time and a few full-time workers, who may become devotees. Variety and creativity are the principal defining criteria separating them from nondevotees in this field. It is one thing to turn a dozen identical pots and quite another to turn a dozen each of which is artistically unique. Those whose sole livelihood comes from the latter are likely to be card-carrying members of the starving artist class; in a world dominated by philistines, sales of artistically different products are relatively infrequent.

Most *product marketing* is the province of organizationally based employees, working in large bureaucracies and constrained there by all sorts of rules and regulations and locked into excessive time demands not of their making. Meanwhile, some small businesses do survive in this field, and offer the product marketers there a devotee occupation. The archetypical example here is the small advertising agency that, similar to the small customs work enterprises, designs and places publicity on a made-to-order basis for customers with budgets so restricted that they are unable to afford the services of bigger companies. Website design and promotion services can also be conceived of as a kind of product marketing. Only two defining criteria appear to separate product marketers in small and large firms, namely control of time and bureaucratic social milieu. These two are nonetheless powerful enough to distinguish devotees from nondevotees in this sphere.

Most *planning work* is likewise bureaucratized in either government or medium-sized business firms. Indeed, city and town planners were listed earlier as professionals. But there are others facets to the occupation of planning that, on the small business level, can generate deep occupational devotion. Here, for instance, is the classificatory home of party and event planners, who if they seek sufficient variety, meet all six defining criteria. The Achilles heel in this business is the level of efficiency of the work team, which if it fails in any major way, could result in disaster for the planner and a concomitant drop in sense of occupational devotion. Thus, it is one thing to plan well for some entertainment during the conference and quite another for the entertainers to fail to show up. Funeral planners suffer similar contingencies, by far the worst being a fumbled casket during the ceremony (Habenstein, 1962, p. 242).

The *family farm* is the final small business considered here. A dwindling phenomenon, to be sure, it still nonetheless offers many owner-families an occupation to which they can become deeply attached. Though they may exploit either plants or animals, the operation must be manageable for the family. All criteria apply here, though some need explaining. Farmers must be innovative when it comes to dealing with untoward pests, weather conditions, government policies, and the like. As for variety they experience it in rotating crops over the years and in observing how each crop grows during a given season. Especially at harvest time, farmers lack control of their own hours and days. But there is usually a lengthy period between growing seasons, when farmers have more control over their own lives. To the extent the farm is also run with hired hands, their level of effectiveness can contribute to or detract from the owner's occupational devotion.

Commitment

Commitment is neither an antecedent nor a concomitant of occupational devotion, but rather one of its most profound consequences. Devotees become committed to a line of work based on their deep involvement in and attachment to its valued core activity. The worker discovers in the course of working just how fulfilling the core tasks can be. This suggests that we must be careful to specify the type of commitment felt, for one type springs from arrangements associated with the job that prove highly costly should the job be abandoned.

Deep involvement in and attachment to a line of activity has been referred to as "value commitment"; it emerges from the many rewards that some workers find in their jobs (Stebbins, 1970b p. 527). Occupational devotees are distinguished by their value commitment to their work, whereas nondevotees, if they are committed at all, experience mostly "continuance commitment" (Becker, 1960; Kantor, 1969; Stebbins, 1970b). Continuance in a role stresses penalties, rather than rewards: it is "the awareness of the impossibility of choosing a different job . . . because of the imminence of social penalties involved in making the switch" (Stebbins, 1970b, p. 527). Workers committed to their jobs primarily by penalties would, if they tried to leave them, face costs like loss of pension, seniority, high salary, and stock option privileges. Some people hang on to their positions in hope of finding a better occupational life upon promotion, possibly even getting put in a devotee work role.

True many occupational devotees would face similar losses were they to try to abandon their work, but such losses are moot since they like it so well that leaving it is unthinkable. These different motivational foundations for value and continuance commitment help explain why people work hard at and often identify with jobs that are not intrinsically devotee, jobs that lack sufficiently alluring core tasks. These workers may report that they are satisfied with their jobs, while being in no position to argue that their jobs are deeply fulfilling.

Values and Occupational Devotion

Commitment is a consequence of occupational devotion, which in turn, is an outcome of the person's steady and, oftentimes, passionate pursuit of certain cultural values. Writing on the theory of American cultural values, Robin Williams (2000, p. 146) lists several that are clearly realizable through occupational devotion, most notably achievement, success, freedom, activity (involvement in something), and individual personality.

Although I know of no research that actually demonstrates that occupational devotees believe they have achieved something important and that they are successful, it seems reasonable to conclude that most would feel precisely this way about these two values. After all, compared with others in their reference groups, they have developed considerable knowledge and skill and acquired considerable experience, all of which they have applied with a certain level of creativity or innovation. But many devotees, unlike some other kinds of workers, cannot measure their achievement and success in remunerative terms, for as observed in chapter 6, high pay by no means always flows from occupational devotion.

Devotee occupations do provide for expression of the value of activity in the form of work, although many other occupations do the same. It is just that the former come without, on balance, significant unpleasant costs, which no small number of nondevotees must bear in order to be active in the realm of work. Thus, assembly line workers are active; they have work, but its core tasks are boring, in part because the skills, knowledge, and experience once required there have been substantially degraded.

Devotee occupations help their workers realize very well the value of individual personality, quite possibly better than any other kind of employment. Devotees are individuated primarily by their exceptional skill, knowledge, and experience as creatively or innovatively manifested in the core tasks of the job. They are further individuated by their social identity as workers in certain prestigious occupations (e.g., the professions, successful small businesses) or in less glamorous ones that are nonetheless seen as solid and respectable, namely, the trades.

Conclusions

This has been, of necessity, a rather sketchy overview of occupational devotion. This necessity is dictated, in part, by the exploratory nature of this inquiry: definition of the occupational devotion itself should, at this stage, be precise enough to delimit the field of study but open enough to new ideas pertinent to it to emerge from research conducted on it. The four types of devotee occupations— liberal professions, consulting/counseling, skilled trades, and small businesses—would seem to encompass the large majority of devotees. But it is certainly possible to have overlooked some devotee occupations that could be classified as small businesses or that could fall entirely outside this typology, as outliers or as specimens of a fifth type. The discovery of these requires further exploration

Well paid occupational devotees help comprise what Richard Florida (2002) describes as the "creative class." But, as will be evident later, not all devotees are highly remunerated, especially those just starting out. Moreover, it is clear that creative people can be employed in situations that fail to engender devotion to their job. At fault here, often, is a social or physical milieu that is inimical to creative work or a set of organizational requirements that removes the control that workers must have over their own time.

Be that as it may, occupational devotion is a real, if not relatively rare, orientation toward work. Furthermore, to understand it well, we must look at both the historical and contemporary background in which it is embedded. The preceding discussion of values motivating such devotion is actually part of that background, but there is much more. Indeed, we could probably find instances of it among the ancients and down through the ages since their time. But, given the scope of this book, such an analysis would take us too far a field. Instead a reasonable starting point in history for examining occupational devotion in modern times would seem to be the rise of the Protestant ethic.

2

Protestant Ethic, Work Ethic, and Occupational Devotion

The Protestant ethic, seldom mentioned today in lay circles and possibly not much discussed there even during its highest point in the seventeenth and eighteenth centuries, has nevertheless been a prominent social force in the development of Western society. Culturally and structurally, this powerful personal orientation among small-enterprise capitalists of the day left its mark, such that it is still being felt in the present. The Protestant ethic is, at bottom, about the will to work.

Following Phillips (2001) my goal in this chapter is to contextualize in social and historical terms, and thereby explain to a certain extent, the trinity of Protestant ethic, work ethic, and occupational devotion and their interrelationship. This approach is basically methodological, in that such contextualization and explanation will by accomplished by framing the discussion in a rich "web of sociological concepts," defined for present purposes as the set of interconnected social science ideas directly related to this special religious orientation. In particular, to provide a sociohistorical background for later analyses of work ethic and occupational devotion, I will explore for new ideas and generalizations about the Protestant ethic using as a sensitizing instrument the conceptual grid developed by Phillips (2001, p. 172, figure 5-1). Table 2.1, which is modeled after Phillips's figure 5-1, contains the main ideas that emerged from my exploration as guided by his grid.

This exploration will also include a look at some of the sociological ramifications of the Protestant ethic as well as some of its economic expressions, as both have been observed in the West. Two main questions will be answered in this chapter, even though only

Table 2.1
Elements of Behavior

		"Head": Beliefs, Ideas	"Heart": Interests, Aspirations	"Hand": Action, Interaction
Construction of Behavior	Social Structures: Shared & Persisting Patterns	Protestant ethic, Work ethic, Leisure is devil's work, Moral norms, Science, Secularization	Eternal salvation, Work (good), Leisure (bad), Leisure (good)	Capitalism, *Nouveaux Riches*, Privilege, Polity, Educations Family, Religion
	Situations: Momentary Behavior in a Scene	Labeling,	Tolerance, Intolerance	Working, Taking leisure, Deviant behavior, Conforming, Moral entrepreneurship
	Individual Structures: Persisting Behavior	Protestant ethic, Work ethic, Workaholism, Occupational devotion	Proof of grace, Wealth, Intrinsic rewards, Extrinsic rewards	Diligence at work, Sloth, Leisure lifestyle, Conspicuous consumption, Work addiction

partial answers are possible at this point: what motivates people to work and how has this motivation changed since the days of the Puritans and, somewhat later, since 1904-1905 when Weber wrote his famous essay?

Max Weber and the Protestant Ethic

Max Weber published, in German in 1904, the first section of his essay "The Protestant Ethic and the Spirit of Capitalism," shortly before he set out to visit the United States. Upon returning at the end of 1904 to his native Germany, he published (in 1905) the second part, which was much informed by his observations on American society and its capitalist economic system. Following Weber's death in 1920 the essay was reprinted, along with a number of lengthier works, in one of several large volumes released in the early 1920s. Not long thereafter, Talcott Parsons translated and published as a book, with direct translation of the title, the only English version of "The Protestant Ethic . . . " (Weber, 1930).

Gerth and Mills (1958, p. 25) said of Weber that "although he was personally irreligious—in his own words, 'religiously unmusical'—he nevertheless spent a good part of his scholarly energy in tracing the effects of religion upon human conduct and life." Weber's treatise on the Protestant ethic and the spirit of capitalism—his most celebrated essay—is, among other things, about individual men (women are never mentioned in the essay) becoming motivated to pursues the value of success and achievement in an occupation defined by each as a divine calling. It is also about how Western capitalism as an economic system (as opposed to great individual undertakings) evolved in part from the activities of these men. Weber was interested in the worldly asceticism of seventeenth and eighteenth century Protestantism, of which Calvinism was the purest instance. In particular he was concerned with Calvin's principle of predestination. Calvin had argued that only a small proportion of all people are chosen for grace, or eternal salvation, whereas the rest are not. This arrangement cannot be changed, for it is God's will.

But, alas, the chosen do not know they have been chosen. The tension of not knowing whether you are among the elect could nevertheless be assuaged in this world by maintaining an implicit trust in Christ, the result of true faith. Moreover, it is a man's duty to consider himself chosen and to act as though this were true, evidence for which came from avoiding worldly temptations like sloth and the hedonic pleasures and from treating work as a calling. A calling—a task set by God but nonetheless chosen by mortals—refers as well to a man's duty to enact his occupational role to the best of his abilities, using his personal powers or material possessions and abstaining from creature pleasures and other leisure activities. This was measured, in part, by usefulness for the community of the goods produced in it. But the most important criterion was found in the realm of capitalist enterprise: amassing wealth through thrift, profit, diligence, investments, sobriety, and similar virtues, and not doing this as an end in-itself. Success and achievement in an occupation, whatever their nature, generate self-confidence, thereby reinforcing a man's belief that he has been chosen. In other words, God helps those who help themselves.

While acknowledging in passing that there were others, Weber concentrated primarily on "callings" or "professions" (referred to in this chapter in modern terms as "occupations") that made it possible to amass wealth. Achieving significant wealth helped generate self-confidence. Hard work, savings, investment, and shrewd decisions in commercial activities all constituted evidence of a man's belief in his own eternal salvation. The result was the emergence of a new social class of self-made entrepreneurs and soon thereafter their integration into the system of Western capitalism as we know it in the present. Weber's object of study were the men who established the family-firm type of capitalist business, common in Western Europe and the United States from the seventeenth century to the present.

According to Cohen (2002, p. 5) Weber was unclear about the relationship between modern capitalist institutions and the Puritans' spirit of capitalism. Still, from his extensive examination of historical evidence, Cohen (2002, p. 254) was able to conclude that "English Puritanism aided capitalism, but its impact was weaker and less dramatic than Weber claimed." Moreover, the impact, attenuated as it was, was primarily cultural, in that helped legitimate further the emerging capitalism of the day and helped mold the broader work ethic as it was taking shape at that time in Occidental culture.

The Protestant Ethic Today

The Protestant ethic, as a summary concept for a distinctive set of motives to work, is largely a dead letter today (it was already in serious decline even at the time Weber wrote about it), though some people still work long hours in pursuit of a variety of more worldly rewards. David Riesman and colleagues (1961) argued that the inner-directed men of the 1950s, who *were* oriented by the Protestant ethic, were being rapidly replaced by other-directed men whose love of mass culture was their singular trait. Otherworldly in orientation as it was, the Protestant ethic, it appears, was nevertheless an important cultural precursor of the modern work ethic. It helped steer the search for the cultural value of activity toward the domain of work (as opposed to that of leisure); work is good and hard work is even better.

Although the Protestant ethic was, in fact, both a cultural and an individual phenomenon, Weber wrote mostly about its psychological side; he looked on the ascetic Protestants as constituting a distinctive type of personality with its own worldview. Analysis of the Protestant ethic as a personal worldview reveals three central components. One is attitude: a person should work, work hard, and avoid leisure as much as possible. The second is value: work activity is good, whereas leisure activity is not. The third component is belief: by hard work people can demonstrate their faith that they number among the chosen. On the macroanalytic level, we find in societies where the Protestant ethic is widely shared that all three personal components are also widely shared. Thus the Protestant ethic is also part of the culture of these societies. And speaking of culture, the Protestant ethic, as mentioned already, also contributed significantly to the rise of the economic system that came to be known as capitalism. That system is now a main social institution in modern Western society.

Social Change

When many individuals are motivated by the Protestant ethic and accumulate wealth according to its dictates, cultural and structural change is bound to occur. Structurally, for example, we have observed the rise of a class of *nouveaux riches* individuals, composed, at least in significant part, of those who have made a great deal of money while inspired by the goal of demonstrating that they were among the elect. Weber, in fact, remarks on just this change during his time. Furthermore, with wealth come certain privileges and hence further structural change (e.g., establishment of private clubs, de facto legal immunity, and special investment opportunities). Structural change following on amassed wealth is further evident in new power relations, as money "talks" through such mechanisms as political parties and philanthropic donations. Thus, in the United States the Republican Party became the voice of the moneyed classes, while Andrew Carnegie and the Rockefeller family, among others, donated large sums to causes they deemed important, at the same time ignoring those they viewed as less significant. Finally structural change is evident in shifts in social status; the new money with obvious links to significant power and privilege climbs ever higher on the ladder of prestige. In Western capitalism, as Veblen (1899) noted, wealth becomes intrinsically honorable; it is viewed as something highly desirable to be emulated by other aspirants to these lofty social heights and, as proof of having it, something to be displayed through conspicuous consumption.

Meanwhile, though the Protestant ethic caused major change, it was also subject to change by powerful external forces. These forces, emanating from change in the institution of work itself, have been profound. More concretely, as the twentieth century unfolded, primary socialization into the work role included less and less reference to the possibility of eternal salvation and the need to prove through diligence on the job that one had been chosen to experience it.

Other external forces that subverted the Protestant ethic included increasing secularization and a growing dominance of science in Western society. Empirical evidence for eternal salvation, difficult to find in any case, has never been a scientific priority. Still, the main principle separating the Protestant ethic from its contemporary expression, the modern work ethic, is precisely that: belief in possible eternal salvation. For in fact, the attitudinal and evaluative components have always been shared by both ethics.

Another reason for the decline of the Protestant ethic is that it never could become the guiding orientation for all paid work, including certain kinds that were carried out even during the heyday of the ethic. True, Weber wrote, albeit briefly, about all callings and the requirement that those pursuing them demonstrate through hard work their chosen place in Heaven. But then he went on to concentrate exclusively on the capitalist trades and the accumulation of wealth in that sphere. Perhaps, for Weber, the problem was that many other occupations fail to produce evidence of diligence so tangible, countable, and incontrovertible as property and monetary riches. As a result, in Weber's day, as in modern times, there were and still are numerous occupations that, at bottom, lie outside the purview of his essay, including those requiring altruistic service to humankind (e.g., nursing, teaching) and extensive development of personal skills and knowledge (e.g., science, the arts).

It is quite possible therefore that, at the time when the Protestant ethic was a prominent motive for many workers, others were enamored instead of occupations with great intrinsic appeal, but which could offer as evidence of having been chosen few convincing ways of publicly displaying diligence and excellence. Put otherwise, these latter occupations were intrinsically attractive, a quality found in the enactment of the work itself rather than in extrinsic rewards it produced such as high remuneration and great profit. It was, in general, difficult to measure, simply and publicly, intrinsic rewards, such that they could constitute proof of the worker's place among the elect. In brief, occupational devotion lay beyond the scope of Weber's essay.

These intrinsically fulfilling occupations falling outside the purview of the Protestant ethic have grown in importance during the twentieth century. And the modern "work ethic," being broader than its religious cousin, the Protestant ethic, finds expression in them as well. What, then, is the work ethic, the ethic that dominates in modern times?

The Work Ethic and Its Variants

By mid-twentieth century the salvation component of the Protestant ethic can be observed, as already noted, only in the outlook of David Riesman's (1956) inner-directed man, who was nevertheless a vanishing breed. What was left by that point in history of the West's distinctive orientation toward work has been known all along simply as the "work ethic." This more diffuse ethic, in fact, shares two of the three components of the Protestant version, mentioned earlier. It shares the same attitudes: a person should work, work hard, and avoid leisure as much as possible. It also shares the same values: work is good, while leisure is not. Only the third component is missing – that of belief: by hard work people can demonstrate their faith that they number among the chosen. In short, the work ethic is but a secular version of the Protestant ethic.

Today's work ethic has been described as "workaholism," an orientation that has probably been around as long as the work ethic itself, and that can be seen as another expression of the Protestant ethic. Marilyn Machlowitz (1980) pioneered this concept, in an attempt to help explain why a conspicuous minority of modern workers, though not guided by the Protestant ethic, are still exceptionally drawn to their work. Part of this attraction is positive, she said; it lies in work's many intrinsic rewards. The other part, however, is negative; that is they are also "work junkies," unfortunates lamentably addicted to their work. These people find joy and fulfillment in their work roles, from which they nonetheless seem compulsively unable to take any real holiday.

The positive, nonaddictive side of workaholism bears a strong resemblance to occupational devotion. Thus the modern work ethic —most generally put that hard work is good—is manifested in at least two main ways among other ways: workaholism and occupational devotion. Generally speaking, the scope of the latter has shrunk in some ways. It has been buffeted by such forces as occupational deskilling and degradation (e.g., Braverman, 1974), industrial restructuring (e.g., downsizing), deindustrialization (e.g., plant closure and relocation), failed job improvement programs (e.g., the Human Relations and Quality of Work movements, Applebaum, 1992, p. 587), and overwork, whether required by employers or sought by workers craving extra income. Nevertheless, certain forms of devotion are more evident today than heretofore, seen for instance, in the rise of the independent consultant and the part-time professional.

But, alas, occupational devotion is a neologism, necessitated partly by the fact that workaholism, as a term, has through careless lay usage become corrupted and distorted to mean, now even for some scientists (e.g., Killinger, 1997; Sonnenberg, 1996), compulsion to work. Perhaps such distortion was to be expected, given that this sense of "ism" refers to the conduct of a class of people seen as much like that of another class, namely, people suffering from alcoholism. In this metaphorical stance compulsive workers, who toil well beyond providing for a reasonable lifestyle, are believed to find little of intrinsic worth in their work, only an irresistible impulse to engage in it. Workaholism will refer in this book only to this negative meaning. These days most people speak most of the time about workaholics as work addicts, either forgetting or overlooking the fact that occupational devotees also exist. Indeed, some of those they casually label workaholic may well be devotees in both thought and action.

In the original, Machlowitzian version of the workaholism thesis, the passion people have for their work is explained, albeit in contradictory terms, by, in part, their love for it and by, in part, their addiction to it. Love suggests workers are attracted to their jobs by such rewards as self-fulfillment, self-expression, self-enrichment, and the like. These lead to deep occupational fulfillment. In contrast, addiction suggests workers are dragged to work by forces beyond their control. No rewards here of the sort just mentioned, rather there is only the compelling need to work and for many to make money, often in amounts well beyond those required for comfortable living. And, over the years, the term workaholism has come to mean exclusively this, with reference to a passion for work having rather quickly fallen into disfavor, perhaps because it so difficult these days to locate instances of it.

In sum, workaholism, occupational devotion, and the work ethic are, with some overlap in meaning, complementary orientations. The work ethic states that work is good, and it is important to do a good job while at it. Workaholism (adulterated version) states that, for some people, working is a compulsion. Occupational devotion includes the condition that work is intrinsically rewarding. The first and third are comprised of both attitudes and values, while the second seriously overextends the first, turning attitude and value into an uncontrollable drive to make money or simply do one's job, if not both. All three orientations, in combination, constitute a substantial replacement of the Protestant ethic.

The Role of Leisure

Neither the Protestant ethic nor the work ethic accords a significant role to leisure. In this regard the first was particularly strict:

The real moral objection is to relaxation in the security of possession, the enjoyment of wealth with the consequence of idleness and the temptations of the flesh, above all of distraction from the pursuit of a righteous life. In fact, it is only because possession involves this danger of relaxation that it is objectionable at all. For the saint's everlasting rest is in the next world; on earth man must, to be certain of his state of grace, "do the works of him who sent him, as long as it is yet day." Not leisure and enjoyment, but only activity serves to increase the glory of God, according to the definite manifestations of His will. (Weber, 1930, p. 157)

Waste of time, be it in sociability, idle talk, luxury, or excessive sleep, was considered the worst of all sins. Bluntly put, unwillingness to work was held as evidence of lack of grace. Sport received a partial reprieve from this fierce indictment, but only so far as it regenerated physical efficiency leading to improved productivity at work (Weber, 1930, p. 167).

By the mid-nineteenth century in Europe and North America leisure had, with the weakening of the Protestant ethic, nonetheless gained a margin of respectability. Gelber (1999, p.1) observed that "industrialism quarantined work from leisure in a way that made employment more work-like and nonwork more problematic. Isolated from each other's moderating influences, work and leisure became increasingly oppositional as they competed for finite hours." Americans, he says, responded in two ways to the threat posed by leisure as potential mischief caused by idle hands. Reformers tried to eliminate or at least restrict access to inappropriate activity, while encouraging people to seek socially approved free-time outlets. Hobbies and other serious leisure pursuits were high on the list of such outlets. In short, "the ideology of the workplace infiltrated the home in the form of productive leisure" (Gelber, 1999, p. 2).

Hobbies were particularly valued, because they bridged especially well the worlds of work and home. And both sexes found them appealing, albeit mostly not the same ones. Some hobbies allowed home bound women to practice, and therefore understand, worklike activities, whereas other hobbies allowed men to create in the female-dominated house their own businesslike space—the shop in the basement or the garage. Among the various hobbies, two types stood out as almost universally approved in these terms: collecting and handicrafts. Still, before approximately 1880, before becoming defined as productive use of free time, these two, along with the other hobbies, were maligned as "dangerous obsessions."

Gelber (1999, pp. 3-4) notes that, although the forms of collecting and craftwork have changed somewhat during the past 150 years, their meaning has remained the same. Hobbies have, all along, been "a way to confirm the verities of work and the free market inside the home so long as remunerative employment has remained elsewhere" (p. 4).

If, in the later nineteenth century, the Protestant ethic was no longer a driving force for much of the working population, its surviving components in the work ethic were. Gary Cross (1990, chap. 7) con-cluded that, during much of this century, employers and upwardly mobile employees looked on "idleness" as threatening industrial development and social stability. The reformers in their midst sought to eliminate this "menace" by, among other approaches, attempting to build bridges to the "dangerous classes" in the new cities and, by this means, to transform them in the image of the middle class. This led to efforts to impose (largely rural) middle-class values on this group, while trying to instill a desire to engage in rational recreation —in modern terms, serious leisure—and consequently to undertake less casual leisure.

But times have changed even more. Applebaum (1992, p. 587) writes that "with increases in the standard of living, consumerism, and leisure activities, the work ethic must compete with the ethic of the quality of life based on the release from work." And as the work ethic withers further in the twenty-first century, in the face of widespread reduction of work opportunities (e.g., Rifkin, 1995; Aronowitz and Difazio, 1994), leisure is slowly, but inexorably it appears, coming to the fore. In other words leisure has, since the middle nineteenth century, been evolving into an institution in its own right. At first, leisure was a poor and an underdevel-oped institution, standing in pitiful contrast next to its robust counterpart of work. But now the twin ideas that work is inherently good and that, when it can be found, people should do it (instead of leisure) are now being increasingly challenged. Beck (2000, p. 125) glimpses the near future as a time when there will still work to be done, but of which a significant portion will be done with-out remuneration:

> The counter-model to the work society is based not upon leisure but upon political freedom; it is a multi-activity society in which housework, family work, club work and voluntary work are prized alongside paid work and returned to the center of public and academic attention. For in the end, these other forms remained trapped inside a value imperialism of work, which must be shaken off.

Beck calls this work without pay "civil labor." Some of it, however, especially club work and voluntary work, is also leisure, for it fits perfectly the definition of "serious leisure" set out in chapter 4: the intensely fulfilling free time activity of amateurs, hobbyists, and skilled and knowledgeable volunteers.

Deviance

The proscription of leisure among those guided by the Protestant ethic provides a textbook example of the way deviance can be generated through labeling and moral entrepreneurship (Becker, 1963). Sociability, idle talk, luxury, and excessive sleep become deviant activities, because they contravene certain moral norms in a community where the most prominent members (the moral entrepreneurs) are trying to prove that they belong in the company of the elect and where the elect are supposed to devote themselves to carrying out God's work on earth. Such work clearly does not include sitting around enjoying oneself.

Yet, this is hardly high criminal behavior, even among seventeenth-century Puritans. That is, it is not of the same moral magnitude as, for example, theft or murder, or in seventeenth-century Massachusetts, adultery, heresy, and witchcraft (Erikson, 1966). Yet, lazy, sociable, and excessively sleepy people were definitely an intolerable lot among the Puritans, even though such people were probably rather numerous. Thus, then as now, some people are unable to work because of accident, old age, or inherited disability. There were probably as well a few souls in the community who could work but refused to do so or do so regularly, and perhaps they were scorned more than the others. Tolerance is an attitude or orientation that we hold toward certain activities or thoughts of others that differ substantially from our own (Stebbins, 1996c, p. 3). It is a passive disposition, falling roughly midway between two active approaches: scorn or disdain toward an activity or thought pattern, on the one hand, and embracement or acceptance of it, on the other.

The ascetic Protestants of the day were not so busy trying to demonstrate their rightful ascent to Heaven that they had no time left for actively scorning behavior that would be tolerated today, if not qualified even more benignly as merely different or eccentric. Erikson (1966, p. 168) reports that people could wind up in court for such transgressions as drinking too much, dressing inappropriately, or letting their hair grow too long. But where the New England Puritans drew the line separating serious intolerable deviance from its less serious cousins was with reference to such "crimes" as heresy and witchcraft. These were viewed as extraordinarily threatening, calling for immediate official adjudication and harsh punishment (e.g., flogging, hanging).

Leisure is no longer deviant, though in many quarters the idea that it is inferior to work clings still. "Every sketch that tries to cross the bridge to the other side of the work society maintains that there is no going beyond. Everything is work, or else it is nothing" (Beck, 2000, p. 63). The two components of the modern work ethic put leisure in its place, as frivolous activity to be enjoyed only after a hard day's work. Nevertheless, as mentioned in the preceding section, the work ethic is falling increasingly out of step with the occupational reality of the early twenty-first century. Much of work, when it can be found, has been trivialized by electronic automation, one important by-product of the Information Age. More and more, and for more and more people, leisure now offers the only hope for finding a deeply interesting and fulfilling existence, though these people must learn that deep interest and fulfillment are found chiefly in amateur, hobbyist, and volunteer activities and not in the casual leisure against which the ascetic Protestants so consistently inveighed.

Institutional Ramifications

The effect of the Protestant ethic has been felt most profoundly in the institutions of work, leisure, economy, and religion. The foregoing discussion has already sketched in some of these effects. Nonetheless, other institutions were also affected by it, even if those effects were less profound. For instance, the families of ascetic Protestants must have been substantially organized around the dictates of the male breadwinner's religious orientation, such that leisure involving him would have been extremely limited. Indeed, he would likely have proscribed leisure for all adult and near-adult members of his family.

Further, since the Protestant ethic was most widely embraced at the time when the great Western democracies were taking root, it is possible that those business people guided by it began to look on government as a means for creating a favorable commercial environment in which to better realize the value of success. Political candidates could well have been assessed by such criteria as their eligibility for grace as well as their inclination to favor business. New business-friendly laws and regulations would have likely been the outcome of these efforts, some of which, in the manner of moral entrepreneurship, were aimed at controlling the kinds of deviance described earlier.

The link between schooling and the Protestant ethic is somewhat more tenuous than the links just made in the polity and the family. Still, a dominant conservative religious outlook in the community might well have influenced curriculum (e.g., no sex education, required reading of religiously compatible literature such as John Bunyan's *The Pilgrim's Progress*). And, quite likely, diligence at schoolwork would have been the order of the day, with little thought given to making learning enjoyable or to fostering pleasure among children either during or after school. The children probably found pleasure, all the same, albeit with scant help from the adults in their lives.

Conclusions

We have scarcely considered all there is to examine relative to the two questions that have guided this chapter: what motivates people to work and how has this motivation evolved since the days of the Puritans and, later, since the years in which Weber wrote his famous essay? Indeed, this inquiry has been constrained by the limited scope of its starting point—the Protestant ethic—the object having been to explore its ramifications down through the centuries. Still, as table 2.1 and Phillips's Web approach show, a great deal of conceptual ground has nevertheless been covered, even if, as it turns out, most of it is either structural or individual. By applying the Web approach, we have learned further that future research into the question of the Protestant ethic and the will to work should attempt to redress this imbalance, by concentrating most heavily on situated behavior.

A number of mainstream sociological concepts guided inquiry in this chapter: work, leisure, social class (the *nouveaux riches*), deviance, conformity, norms, and secularization. Then, to broaden the analysis, I added to this foundation several more specialized concepts, among them intrinsic and extrinsic reward, conspicuous consumption, moral entrepreneurship, work ethic, and Protestant ethic. At the most basic level, however, I examined a list of society's usual social institutions to determine which applied to the two questions. Accordingly, discussion centered in diverse ways on the institutions of religion, social control, economy, polity, family, work, and leisure. Finally, a few concepts in table 2.1 are really little more than commonsense ideas, most notably sloth, wealth, and grace.

It has been informative to look on contemporary Western society from the standpoint of the Protestant ethic and its ramifications as they have been felt over the years. First, this analysis has given historical depth to our understanding of the modern work ethic, at a time when it faces even greater challenges in the Information Age of the twenty-first century. Likewise, we have added historical depth to our understanding of the role of leisure vis-à-vis work, accomplished in the main by charting the way that leisure has been slowly but surely inching its way toward center stage, a place once reserved solely for work. The future augurs well for an even balance in the importance of the two for some people and an imbalance skewed toward leisure for many others. Those favoring work over leisure will be but a small minority, composed mainly of occupational devotees and stressed-out workaholics.

Second, this analysis exemplifies the extent to which we in the West have passed from a sacred to a secular society. For the vast majority of people here work has little or nothing to do with the next world, unless of course, it is religious work. The social and psychological milieu of the ascetic Protestant, rooted as it was in small rural communities of another era, was the antithesis of the sensual, increasingly leisure oriented world of the urbanized worker of modern times.

Third, what constitutes deviance has also changed enormously from the Puritan era to the present. One reason for this change has been the growth of tolerance. Indeed, widespread tolerance, it appears, is characteristic only of the modern age (Tinder, 1975, p. 7). The generalized tolerance of religious, political, ethnic, and deviant differences is one of the concomitants of developments in science and technology, the growth of commerce and capitalism, the move toward representative government, the decline of absolutism, the trend toward a more global viewpoint, and the contact of diverse cultures (Barnes, 1965, chap 18). The ascetic Protestants were highly intolerant, modern Western man is, with some unsettling exceptions, significantly less so.

Today, the Protestant ethic is, as I have said, a dead letter. Occasionally, a person describes another as a hard worker imbued with this orientation, but such comments are becoming more infrequent with each passing year. Perhaps, too, these comments seem to come mostly from older people who still remember hearing about the Protestant ethic, even if, in their present-day application of it, they really have in mind nothing more than the broader, but simpler, idea of the work ethic. Does anyone really think today that a person's hard work springs from his desire to demonstrate his election in the hereafter? Be that as it may, the Protestant ethic was an important link in the chain of social conditions that led to the rise of Western capitalism and a significant influence in framing the work ethic as we now know it. On the whole, it appears that we are better off having passed through this phase of human social development, as extended as it has been.

3

Gender, Family, Social Class,
and Social Character

So far we have framed occupational devotion in four broad social contexts: history, religion, work, and to some extent, leisure, with much more to be said on the last of these in the next chapter. This does not, however, exhaust all the angles from which we can look on this orientation and thereby better understand its fit in the larger society in which it is expressed. Four additional angles are considered in this chapter: gender, family, social class, and social character. Each enables us to see another side of occupational devotion in comparison with other orientations toward work. We turn first to gender.

Gender

The goal in this section is to look at the devotee occupations through the lens of gender status and gender relations to identify differences in orientation that prevail in this sphere. Because so little research exists on this subject, the present effort must be understood as little more than an attempt to sensitize the reader to various research possibilities and to the general relationship pertaining between gender and occupational devotion. We will proceed in this exploratory vein along lines of the six criteria for determining devotee occupations, which were presented in chapter 1. Statements made in this section about proportions of males and females in those occupations are based on tabulated data published in the *Statistical Abstract of the United States* (U.S. Census Bureau, 2000, pp. 416-418).

Applying the first of the six criteria–skill, knowledge, and experience–there appears, generally speaking, to be no gender differences in this regard, in that both sexes are capable of acquiring these for all, or nearly all, devotee occupations. Admittedly, discriminatory practices sometimes prevent women from, for example, entering training programs traditionally seen as for men only. Indeed social and cultural arrangements of considerable diversity, rather than innate capacity, may work to constrain female pursuit of education for and employment in certain devotee occupations. More will be said on this matter later in this section.

Likewise, desire for variety in work tasks appears, given lack of evidence to the contrary, to be as important for one sex as the other. Nor is there any reason to believe that the sexes would be differentiated according to this criterion. But there is likely substantial differentiation along lines of the third criterion: creativity and innovation. Why? Certainly men and women are equally capable of doing both. Probably so, but not likely always in the same ways. If nothing else their different life experiences and situations, forced on them by the circumstances in which they live, should result in different ways of seeing the world, in general, and their devotee occupations, in particular.

Let us look an example from professional stand-up comedy. In Western society men are usually much more comfortable using off-color humor in public than women. Thus

> most females in comedy struggle with the question of whether to work blue [use off-color jokes and language]. For them, working blue is not an extension of street life, as it is for many men, but rather an attempt, made in the interest of success, to be like male comics who appear to be succeeding on account of dick jokes [dirty jokes]. Many amateur and early professional females wrestle with this problem: whether to retain their femininity and risk failure, or renounce it in certain ways and increase the chances of success. (Stebbins, 1990, pp. 103-104)

Female comics who opt for retaining their femininity must, as a consequence, be inventive; they must find ways of being funny that are uncommon in a field dominated by men who, as early professionals, often rely on blue humor.

Quite possibly the most profound difference between the sexes in occupational devotion becomes evident when we apply the criterion of aptitude and taste for particular activities. Whether socialized or inherited or influenced by a combination of both, men and women as groups do sometimes vary quite dramatically along these lines. One of the most celebrated of these differences is the male tendency to be endowed with stronger mathematical abilities and the female tendency to be endowed with stronger verbal abilities (Mackie, 1991, pp. 38-39). Of course we should not forget that these are differences in group averages and that, as a consequence, many an individual man and woman falls above or below the mean level for their group. To the extent they have little aptitude or taste for these specialties, men would be less inclined than women to seek work in languages and women less inclined than men to seek work in mathematics (e.g., women account for 31.1 percent of mathematical and computer scientists).

Aptitude has to do with natural abilities and propensities, whereas taste, we generally assume, is socialized. Part of this socialization includes learning to distinguish what society considers men's and women's work (Jacobs, 2003, p.33). Men and women share many tastes for devotee work in small business, consulting and counseling, and the liberal professions. Only in the skilled trades do noticeable gender differences appear, doing so across the entire category with women accounting for only 2.5 percent of all construction workers. Thus it is rare to encounter a female plumber, carpenter, or electrician, even if training programs in these fields are formally as available to them as to men.

But if both men and women are widely distributed throughout the professions, this distribution is nevertheless uneven. Though there are a few males among them, 92.9 percent of registered nurses are female. It is much the same for social workers (71.4 percent are female). My understanding here is that, these days, taste, possibly even more than discrimination, keeps most women from such devotee occupations as mechanical engineering (7.1 percent) and airline piloting (3.1 percent). Thus, Gignac (2003), reporting on data collected by the Canadian Informational Processing Society, says that women are avoiding computer science programs because of "negative stereotypes" they have about the nature of computer work and the people it attracts (e.g., the geek). To the extent that consulting and counseling are extensions of organized professional work, the same observations pertain here as well. There are, to be sure, many other factors than taste that lead to job segregation along sex lines, an examination of which would, however, take us far from the present discussion (for a review of these see Jacobs, 2003, pp. 34-35).

Both men and women are well represented in all eleven small business categories, even though within some categories, certain kinds of enterprise hold greater interest for one sex than the other. Although I have no readily available statistics, it appears that men predominate in the funeral planning and flying instruction businesses. In custom work, women seem to abound in floral arrangement, but show little taste for the male preserve of tattooing (Atkinson, 2003). By contrast, few men seek a career in child day care, whereas for many women, it offers highly desirable work (98.4 percent of pre-kindergarten and kindergarten workers are female). It might be argued here that the low pay that goes with this service discourages many men and even some women from becoming involved in it. Yet, men are found in significant numbers among the starving artists and the chefs of small *haute cuisine* restaurants, work that is often far more a labor of love than one of financial profit.

Disagreeable social milieux may well account for some differential attraction among men and women to devotee occupations. For instance, a sexist atmosphere in a small engineering firm could well discourage qualified women from accepting a job there, and some men might feel uncomfortable being employed in the female-dominated, hospital nursing profession. Nor does the physical milieu of devotee occupations always meet with universal enthusiasm. Being on a farm excites some people, but not most city slickers. The outdoor work of the forester has its devotees, but many are those who prefer an environment free of insects and extremes in weather of, say, an office or a shop. And employment data do suggest that the physical environment may itself be a matter of taste. At least women are poorly represented in such outdoor occupations as farming, forestry, and fishing, where they may also find unappealing the occasionally heavy requirements of such work.

Control of time–the sixth criterion–does sometimes affect quite dramatically and differentially the attraction men and women have for a particular devotee occupation. Women, many of whom must juggle the demands of child rearing with those of work have as a result a greater interest than many men in flexible work schedules and flexible work locations, and may well feel they must eschew occupations that fail to offer them. The consulting and counseling trades beckon for this very reason, and accordingly, women predominate in, for example, education and vocational counseling (68.7 percent). Such work may require the worker to go somewhere to meet with clients, gather data, and perhaps present a report, but most of the time much of it can be done at home or, according to a convenience schedule, at an office. Here, in the interstices of tending to family obligations, the worker can analyze her data and write her reports fired by the enthusiasm of a true devotee.

Part-time work in all four types of devotee occupations offers a similar advantage of flexibility, although in some instances, the worker may still have to meet a schedule that could disadvantage housebound mothers. Small devotee businesses enabling a mother to work from her home are likewise prized for their flexibility. These include artistic craftwork, family farming, and such custom work as tailoring and hair styling. It is also possible to operate from home a personal coaching service or a small-scale party and event-planning enterprise.

Do men and women differentially embrace the five values? Some of the observations made in this section that were centered on the six criteria suggest the answer to this question is no. Common sense–and there seems to be little else to go on here–also suggests that success, achievement, freedom of action, individual personality, and activity are equally prized by both sexes, even if the two may sometimes diverge in the ways that men and women prefer to realize each in their everyday work lives. For instance, we shall in the next section that, more so than male devotees, females devotees strive to realize their value of freedom of action by searching for flexibility in the hours and places of their work.

Family

The lifestyle of the occupational devotee, including its family component, is considered in a later chapter. In this section we look at the family as context for occupational devotion, for those devotees who have partners, spouses, and perhaps children. Whereas by no means all devotees are recluses, is quite possible that research will one day reveal that, because of the intense appeal of their work, many fail to develop enduring relationships of the familial kind.

The literature on workaholism, some of which was reviewed in the preceding chapter, is replete with lengthy discussions of the negative impact that highly committed workers have on their families. Whether motivated by value commitment or continuance commitment, people given to long hours of work have, obviously, less time to see their families than those who work shorter hours. Note, too, that leisure, both serious and casual, is also capable of drawing members away from the family circle for substantial periods of time (e.g., Gillespie, Leffler, and Lerner, 2002). Occupational devotion, like its serious leisure counterpart, seems for many enthusiasts to know no boundaries; it is difficult to control, to call it quits for the day or the week. It seems that no one wants to stop when having fun.

For devotees who have them their families can be, and in fact probably are, their biggest cheering section. The reasons for this are legion. One, the family, which is often cut from the same cultural cloth, is likely to subscribe to the same values as the devotee: success, freedom, achievement, activity through work, and individual personality. That one of their number realizes these in exceptional ways is cause for group pride and celebration.

Two, adult family members satisfied with their lot in life, a major segment of which is work, are usually easygoing people both on and of the job. It can happen, then, that a quid pro quo of sorts is struck, in which the family supports the devotee in return for the latter's equanimity in family matters. Certainly, the devotee's disposition at home is going to be different from that of the typical nondevotee, where the first basks in the warmth of his deeply fulfilling work and second squirms with dread at the thought of having to go next day to the office or plant.

Three, the large majority of devotee occupations are broadly humanitarian, in the sense that each contributes in its own fashion to human well being. That is, they serve humankind in a variety of beneficial ways. True, members of any occupation can through dishonesty exploit clients, bosses, customers, or co-workers, but generally the devotee occupations serve rather than exploit. This is part of what makes them so immensely attractive and respectable. A person cannot be a devotee of work that requires, for instance, systematically lying to customers. Such work includes the proverbial sellers of "pre-owned" cars and the designers of intentionally misleading advertising. Journalists who are required to slant their stories to fit the moral and political biases of the owner of their magazine or newspaper constitute another example. Knowing the great extent and effect of exploitative work in modern life makes it difficult on moral grounds for a family to argue against activity of one of its members that, be it work or leisure, supports humanitarian causes and principles.

There is no doubt that the occupational devotee benefits enormously from family support. The old adage that behind every successful man there is a woman attests to this observation, although it also happens these days that a successful woman is sometimes backed by a man. The chapter on lifestyle will look into the ways in which domestic life can get substantially organized around the devotee's work interests. Suffice it to note here that, for devotees who have a family of some kind, it generally seems to function in their occupational interest, sometimes, perhaps even oftentimes, at the expense of the interests of other family members. World-renowned accident reconstruction specialist Rod Davis explains:

> "Your family pays–especially my family. Especially with me teaching all over Canada and abroad, with the responsibilities I had with the police service. I was away an awful lot," says Davis, who smiles at his wife Karen as they sit in their living room.
> "My success has been as a result mostly of the contributions and support that I've had from my family–particularly Karen," he says. "Karen, God bless you. The phone was always at your side. I don't know how many phone calls you've taken over the years in the middle of the night."
> "Says Karen, No matter where we went, he had to be ready."
> "A lot of hockey games missed," adds their son Mathew.
> "A lot of hockey games," Dad agrees. "A lot of baseball games, a lot of figure skating for my daughter (Stephanie). A lot of sacrifice I think most people don't understand." (Slobodian, 2003, p. D4)

Social Class

The assumption, set out in chapter 1, that the work to which a person is devoted carries with it a respectable personal and social identity, has direct import for social class. It was noted in the same chapter, however, that positive identification with the job is not a defining condition of occupational devotion, since such identification can develop for other reasons, such as high salary, prestige of employer, or advanced educational qualifications. Nevertheless, this suggests that, when it comes to occupational devotion, social class as measured by prestige of the work provides its own prism through which to view such devotion.

Partial support for this proposition comes from research on serious leisure, where the reward of favorable self-image emanating from earnestly pursuing a serious leisure activity has been found to be of relative minor importance when viewed against the rewards experienced from executing the activity itself (e.g., rewards of self-expression, self-actualization). True, pursuit of either the serious leisure activity or the devotee occupation must be seen as respectable by the enthusiast's reference groups, but typically, acquiring respectability remains as only a secondary motive underlying the pursuit—in other words, it is not part of the set of core tasks.

This helps explain why some devotee occupations, though not as prestigious as some others in this kind of work, are still vigorously sought after. The skilled trades lack the prestige of the liberal professions, but are for all that hardly short on recruits who see them as properly dignified. Put otherwise, along the prestige dimension of social stratification, trades workers fall into a lower class than professionals, but that appears to in no way diminish the appeal of craftwork as a distinctive set of tasks.

Much the same observation can be made for the power dimension of social stratification; Craft workers, though anything but collectively weak given their unionization, for example, still fail to approach the high degree of power enjoyed in professional circles. But, as before, seeking and retaining power are not central goals in devotee occupations, at least compared with the powerful goal of pursuing highly interesting work. No matter that, in this regard, they are of somewhat lower social class in terms of power; it is the profoundly intriguing and fulfilling nature of the work that really counts.

This brings us to the third classic dimension of social stratification, namely, economic status. It is the most problematic of the three. Indeed, so much so that a separate chapter (chap. 6) has been set aside to deal with it. The problem we will tackle there revolves around the way high remuneration can become a powerful incentive in its own right, so powerful that sometimes it even undermines occupational devotion. Suffice it to say in this section that, from the standpoint of social stratification, unionized tradesmen seem to enjoy reasonably high levels of income, so high that they may well spark a certain degree of envy among some small business proprietors and even some junior consultants, counselors, and professionals. On this dimension, then, they rank much nearer the top (relative to other devotee occupations) compared with their location on the dimensions of prestige and power.

Social Character

An examination of the several analyses of American character—whose heyday ran from approximately the 1950s through the 1970s—

revealed only one study that even touched on occupational devotion. That study was evidently not, for example, William Whyte's *The Organization Man* (Whyte, 1956), which bore on the many American workers who, at the time, were seeking and finding economic and personal security by conforming to the dictates of large organizations of various sorts. For occupational devotion thrives in, at most, a lightly bureaucratized work milieu that encourages creativity and innovation. Nor was it Philip Slater's *The Pursuit of Loneliness* (Slater, 1970), an exploration of American acquisitiveness and its failure to bring happiness and peace of mind to consumers.

The study that did have something to say about occupational devotion (though this expression was never used there) was that of David Riesman who, with Reuel Denney and Nathan Glazer, published in 1950 a highly influential examination of American character by the title of *The Lonely Crowd*, followed in 1961 by an updated version (Riesman, 1961). Although other books followed, centered primarily on either American character or higher education, Riesman's reputation as a scholar remained closely tied to this, his first book.

The Lonely Crowd was an impressionistic study of work and leisure, a report of the experiences of the three authors "of living in America–the people we have met, the jobs we have held, the books we have read, the movies we have seen, and the landscape" (Riesman, 1961, p. xlix). *Faces in the Crowd* (Riesman, 1952), was more empirically sound, based as it was on systematic interviews with a broad ranging sample of Americans. Nonetheless, many of the ideas presented in *The Lonely Crowd*, because of their face validity, found in the United States widespread acceptance in scholarly and popular circles alike.

The most celebrated of these ideas are the three types of directedness labeled "inner," "other," and "tradition." Tradition-directed people resist much of social change, conforming through inculcated rules to the dictates of clan, age, sex group, and the like. Tradition-direction was relatively uncommon in mid-twentieth-century America (and it still is), since long before, it had largely been superceded by the other two types. Inner-direction rests much less on group dictates and more on personal goals and interests, particularly fame, wealth, and achievement. The inner-directed personality is often driven by the Protestant ethic. But even inner-direction was becoming less common in the 1950s, as the other-directed, consumer personality began gaining ascendancy. Self-control for other-directed people–the new, moneyed, middle class—lies outside the self in their social relations with others in the community. Riesman and his colleagues held that the three types find fullest expression in the world of leisure, where inner-directed people value achievement-based hobby, amateur, or volunteer activities vis-à-vis other-directed people who typically go in for mass leisure. But, for the latter, such leisure draws mostly people like themselves, in the course of which they lose their identity and become lost in the lonely crowd.

The Lonely Crowd stirred great intellectual interest in mass culture and leisure, albeit not always in a scientifically sound manner. In his preface to the 1961 edition, Riesman lamented that some professional social scientists concluded that the generalizations presented there could be "regarded as proven" (p. xvi), even though their authors intended they be seen only as hypotheses. The book's tentativeness did not weaken its impact, however: it numbers among the finest studies of American work and leisure considered together.

And what about occupational devotion in all this? The inner-directed personalities are clearly the most likely of the three types to have discovered it in their work, even if the Riesman team, as others have since (see chapter 2), sometimes confused such devotion with the Protestant ethic. Inner-directed people easily meet a number of the six defining criteria. They value the accumulation of skill, knowledge, and experience in both work and leisure (they prefer the serious kind) and the sense of achievement accompanying this. Moreover, since they are the least likely of the three types to rely on group dictates, they should be the most likely to be creative or innovative and be in control of their own time. And that personal goals and interests are foremost among the inner-directed, suggests that they seek and find devotee work befitting their peculiar aptitudes and tastes. As for the other two criteria–variety and social and physical milieu–*The Lonely Crowd* does not supply enough information on these conditions to allow for their application.

The tradition-directed man is, quite obviously, most unlikely to become an occupational devotee. Even rarer now than in Riesman's day, he lacks the necessary commitment to the value of individual personality that propels occupational devotees and the inner-directed people with the same bent. And in a way, the same is true for the other-directed type, who however, dances to whatever tune the contemporary crowd is playing. Again, there is scant individualism in this, only conformity to mass interests. Occupational devotion, for reasons of taste and available time, pushes the devotee to avoid extensive routine involvement in superficial, casual leisure.

But what about interests in fame and wealth said by Riesman and his colleagues to inspire the inner-directed type? Such interests are difficult to reconcile with the present conceptualization of occupational devotion, the most important goals of which are finding high attraction to core work tasks and savoring the senses of success and achievement that come with carrying out those tasks. The Riesman team never studied how inner-directed people rank, according to their importance, the desiderata of fame, wealth, and achievement. Nonetheless, research in serious leisure suggests that, compared with achievement, fame, really a part of identity and self-image, is but a secondary reward, while remuneration, when it occurs, an even more distant one. The importance of wealth for the devotee is taken up in chapter 6.

Conclusions

To this point discussion has centered primarily on work, its relatively uncommon expression as occupational devotion, its roots in the Protestant ethic, and its historical transformation as manifested in workaholism and the contemporary work ethic. We have, in the present chapter, extended this contextual analysis to include the domains of gender, family, social class, and social character, so that occupational devotion now no longer appears as an isolated orientation but rather one deeply and uniquely embedded in the history and social and cultural arrangements of modern society.

This brings us to the point where we must address ourselves to the other principal focus of this book: leisure. In the next chapter we look at, always in parallel with work, the three main types of serious leisure, their motivational basis, and their evolution over approximately the past century and a half. The diverse ways in which these types relate to occupational devotion are then spelled out in chapter 5.

4

Serious Leisure

During the past century and a half or so, the three main types of serious leisure have also been significantly influenced by the multitude of forces considered in earlier chapters. But those forces have affected activities that have been undertaken in an atmosphere very different from that of work, namely the atmosphere of serious leisure, which is characterized by, for example, significantly greater flexibility, openness, experimentation, and lack of coercion. Moreover, work habits and attitudes adapted to leisure can, when refracted back onto work, reveal some important qualities of work undertaken as a livelihood, most notably the devotee occupations. And, of course, serious leisure has its special properties, which are not adaptations from work, but which can nonetheless inform us about work itself.

The two principal goals of this chapter, then, are first to present historical sketches of the three main types of serious leisure and, next, to examine their motivational foundation. We start, nonetheless, with a look at the serious leisure perspective.

Serious Leisure

The term "serious leisure" made its debut in social science circles in 1982. The initial statement (Stebbins, 1982) and several more recent ones bearing on the nature of serious leisure, are now reasonably well expressed in what seems to have become the standard abbreviated definition of this type of activity. Serious leisure is the systematic pursuit of an amateur, hobbyist, or volunteer activity that participants find so substantial and interesting that, in the typical case, they launch themselves on a career centered on acquiring and expressing its special skills, knowledge, and experience (Stebbins, 1992, p. 3). Because of the widespread tendency to see the idea of career as applying only to occupations, note that, in this definition, the term is used much more broadly, following Goffman's (1961a, pp. 127-128) elaboration of the idea of "moral career." Broadly conceived, careers are available in all substantial, complicated roles, including especially those in work, leisure, deviance, politics, religion, and interpersonal relationships (see also, Lindesmith, Strauss, and Denzin, 1999, pp. 315-316; Hewitt, 1991, p. 246). As for the definition just presented, it is probably as good a depiction of this form of leisure as can be presented in a one-sentence definition.

Note, too, that here the adjective "serious" embodies such qualities as earnestness, sincerity, importance, and carefulness, rather than those of gravity, solemnity, joylessness, distress, and anxiety. Although the second set of terms occasionally describe serious leisure events, they are uncharacteristic of them and fail to nullify, or, in many instances, even dilute, the overall fulfillment gained by the participants. Here "serious" is fundamentally a folk term, an adjective the people I interviewed frequently used to distinguish their kind of leisure from casual leisure. The most recent discussion of the (largely) exploratory research from which the serious leisure perspective emerged is available in Stebbins (2001a, chap. 8).

To sharpen our understanding of serious leisure, it is commonly contrasted with "casual" or "unserious" leisure, or the immediately intrinsically rewarding, relatively short-lived pleasurable activity requiring little or no special training to enjoy it (Stebbins, 1997a). Among its types are play (including dabbling), relaxation (e.g., sitting, napping, strolling), passive entertainment (e.g., TV, books, recorded music), active entertainment (e.g., games of chance, party games), sociable conversation, and sensory stimulation (e.g., sex, eating, drinking). It is considerably less substantial, and offers no career of the sort just described for serious leisure. Casual leisure can also be defined residually as all leisure not classifiable as amateur, hobbyist, or career volunteering. Despite the seemingly trivial nature of most casual leisure, I will argue later that it is nonetheless important in personal and social life.

The Nature of Serious Leisure

To gain a more complete understanding of serious leisure, we must move beyond our handy but nonetheless limited one-sentence definition to look more closely at its three basic types. Amateurs are found in art, science, sport, and entertainment, where they are inevitably linked in several ways with their professional counterparts. For their part, the professionals are identified and defined according to theory developed in the social scientific study of professions, a substantially more exact procedure than the ones relying on simplistic and not infrequently commercially shaped common sense images of these workers. In other words, when studying amateurs and professionals descriptive definitions turn out to be too superficial, such as observing that the activity in question constitutes a livelihood for the second but not the first or that the second works fulltime at it whereas the first pursues it part-time. Rather, we get much closer to the essence of both ideas by noting, for example, that the two are locked in and therefore defined by a system of relations linking professionals, amateurs, and their publics ("the P-A-P system") that is too complex to be described here. (This definition and one based on attitudinal differences are discussed in greater detail in Stebbins 1979; 1992, chap. 3.)

Hobbyists lack this professional alter ego, even if they sometimes have commercial equivalents and often have small publics who take an interest in what they do. Hobbyists can be classified according to one of five categories: collectors, makers and tinkerers, activity participants (in noncompetitive, rule-based, pursuits), players of sports and games (where no professional counterparts exist), and enthusiasts in one of the liberal arts. Fishing (Yoder, 1997), bushwalking (Hamilton-Smith, 1993), and barbershop singing (Stebbins, 1996a) exemplify the third, bound as they are by certain cultural and regulatory norms, while curling (Apostle, 1992), long-distance running (Yair, 1990), and competitive swimming (Hastings, Kurth, Schloder, and Cyr, 1995) exemplify the fourth, which are bound by the rules of the game. Liberal arts hobbyists are enamored of their systematic quest for knowledge for its own sake (Stebbins, 1994). This is typically accomplished by reading voraciously in a field of art, sport, cuisine, language, culture, history, science, philosophy, politics, or literature.

Volunteers, the third basic type, engage in volunteering, defined here as uncoerced help offered either formally or informally with no or, at most, token pay for the benefit of both other people and the volunteer (see Graham and Stebbins, 2004 for further discussion of this definition). It should be noted, however, that the field of career volunteering is narrower, even if it does cover considerable ground. One taxonomy, consisting of sixteen types of formal, organizational volunteering, shows the wide scope of career volunteering. Career volunteers provide a great variety of services in education, science, civic affairs (advocacy projects, professional and labor organizations), spiritual development, health, economic development, religion, politics, government (programs and services), human relationships, recreation, and the arts. Some of these volunteers work in the fields of safety or the physical environment, while others prefer to provide necessities (e.g., food, clothing, shelter) or support services. Although much of career volunteering appears to be connected in some way with an organization of some sort, the scope of this leisure is possibly even broader, perhaps including the kinds of helping (informal volunteering) devoted individuals do for social movements or for neighbors and family. Still, the definition of serious leisure restricts attention everywhere to volunteering in which the participant can find a career, in which they find more or less continuous and substantial involvement, rather than one-time or occasional donations of money, blood, services, and the like (Stebbins, 1996b).

Making a case for volunteering as leisure—as opposed to the far more common definition of it as unpaid work or unpaid productive activity—poses little logical difficulty. For the word to remain etymologically consistent with its Latin roots, it must be seen, as all leisure is, as uncoerced activity. Moreover, as all leisure, leisure volunteering must be seen as basically either fulfilling or enjoyable experience (if not both), for otherwise we are forced to posit that volunteers are somehow pushed into performing their roles by circumstances they would prefer to avoid, a contradiction of terms.

Serious leisure is further defined by six distinctive qualities, which are found among amateurs, hobbyists, and volunteers alike. One is the occasional need to *persevere*, as seen in confronting danger (e.g., in eating wild mushrooms and climbing mountains, Fine and Holyfield, 1996), managing stage fright (e.g., when participating in theater and sport, Stebbins, 1981) or suffering embarrassment (e.g., while doing volunteer work, Floro, 1978, p. 198). Yet, it is clear that positive feelings about the activity come, to some extent, from sticking with it through thick and thin, from conquering adversity. A second quality is, as indicated earlier, that of finding a *career* in the endeavor, shaped as it is by its own peculiar contingencies, turning points and stages of achievement and involvement.

Most, if not all, careers in serious leisure owe their existence to its third quality: serious leisure participants make a significant personal *effort* based on specially acquired *knowledge, training, or skill,* and, indeed at times, all three. Examples include such achievements as showmanship, athletic prowess, scientific knowledge, and long experience in a role. Fourth, a number of *durable benefits, or outcomes,* of serious leisure have so far been identified, mostly from research on amateurs and hobbyists. They include self-actualization, self-enrichment, self-expression, regeneration or renewal of self, feelings of accomplishment, enhancement of self-image, social interaction and belongingness, and lasting physical products of the activity (e.g., a painting, scientific paper, piece of furniture). A further benefit—self-gratification, or the combination of superficial enjoyment and deep fulfillment—is to the extent that the component of enjoyment dominates, also one main benefit of casual leisure.

The fifth quality—participants in serious leisure tend to *identify* strongly with their chosen pursuits—springs from the presence of the other five. In contrast, casual leisure, although hardly humiliating or despicable, is nonetheless usually too fleeting, mundane, and commonplace for most people to find a distinctive identity there. I imagine that this was the quality Cicero had in mind when he coined his famous slogan: *Otium cum dignitate,* or leisure with dignity.

The sixth quality of serious leisure is the *unique ethos* that grows up around each expression of it. The central component of this ethos is the special social world that develops when enthusiasts in a particular field pursue over many years their interests in it. Unruh (1979, p. 115) defines social world as:

> a unit of social organization which is diffuse and amorphous. . . . Generally larger than groups or organizations, social worlds are not necessarily defined by formal boundaries, membership lists, or spatial territory. . . . A social world must be seen as an internally recognizable constellation of actors, organizations, events, and practices which have coalesced into a perceived sphere of interest and involvement for participants. Characteristically, a social world lacks a powerful centralized authority structure and is delimited by . . . effective communication and not territory nor formal group membership.

In a later paper, Unruh (1980) added that social worlds are characterized by voluntary identification, by a freedom to enter into and depart from them. Moreover, because they are so diffuse, it is common for members to be only partly involved in all the activities they have to offer. After all, a social world may be local, regional, multiregional, national, even international. Third, people in complex societies are often members of several social worlds, with only some being related to leisure. Finally, social worlds are held together, to an important degree, by semiformal, or "mediated communication." They are rarely heavily bureaucratized, yet because of diffuseness, they are rarely characterized by intense face-to-face interaction. Rather, communication is typically mediated by newsletters, posted notices, telephone messages, and mass mailings as well as by Internet communications, radio and television announcements, and similar means. And there is the ever-stronger possibility that the Internet will, in future, become the most popular of these.

Every social world contains four types of members: strangers, tourists, regulars, and insiders (Unruh, 1979; 1980). Strangers are intermediaries who normally participate little in the leisure activity itself, but who nonetheless do something important to make it possible by, for example, managing municipal parks (in amateur baseball), minting coins (in hobbyist coin collecting), or organizing the work of teachers' aids (in career volunteering). Tourists are temporary participants in a social world; they have come on the scene momentarily for entertainment, diversion, or profit. Most amateur and hobbyist activities have publics of some kind, which are, in this conceptualization, constituted of tourists. The clients of many volunteers can be similarly classified. Regulars routinely participate in the social world; in serious leisure, they are the amateurs, hobbyists, and volunteers themselves. Insiders are those among them who show exceptional devotion to the social world they share, to maintaining it, to advancing it, and to displaying excellence there. In the studies of amateurs, such people were analyzed as "devotees," who are highly dedicated to their pursuit, and contrasted with "participants," or regulars, who are moderately dedicated to it (Stebbins, 1992, pp. 46-48).

Missing from Unruh's conceptualization of the social world, but nonetheless vitally important for the study of serious leisure, is the observation that an evolved subculture is to be found there as well, one function of which is to interrelate the "diffuse and amorphous constellations." Consequently, it should be noted that members find associated with each social world a unique set of special norms, values, beliefs, lifestyles, moral principles, performance standards, and similar shared representations. Only by taking these elements into account can we logically speak about, for example, social stratification in social worlds. This Unruh does when differentiating insiders from regulars, and I just did for serious leisure by differentiating devotees from participants.

In addition to my own work, empirical validation of these six distinctive qualities comes from several studies (e.g., Parker, 1996; McQuarrie and Jackson, 1996; Siegenthaler and Gonsalez, 1997; Nichols and King, 1999; Arai 2000).

The Rise of Amateurism

As professionalization spreads from one occupation to another, what was once considered play in some of these spheres is evolving quietly, inevitably, and unnoticeably into a new form—one best named *modern amateurism*. Modern amateurism has been raising alongside those occupations where some participants in the occupation are now able to make a substantial living from it and, consequently, to devote themselves to it as a vocation rather than an avocation. Although there are possibly others, we can label science, entertainment, sport and games, as well as fine arts, as the major occupational areas where work was once purely play and where modern amateurism is now a parallel development.

What has been happening is that those who play at the activities encompassed by these occupations are being overrun in significance, if not in numbers, by professionals and amateurs. It is a process that seems to unfold as follows. As opportunities for full-time pursuit of a skill or activity gradually appear, those people with even an average aptitude for such skills are able to develop them to a level observably higher than that of the typical part-time participant. With today's mass availability of professional performances (or products), whatever the field, new standards of excellence soon confront all participants, professional or not. Although the performances of professionals are frequently impressive, no category of participant is more impressed than that of nonprofessionals who, through direct experience, know the activity intimately. Indeed, once they become aware of professional standards, all they have accomplished seems mediocre by comparison. They are thus faced with a critical choice in their careers as participants: either they restrict identification with the activity so as to remain largely unaffected by such invidious comparisons, or they identify sufficiently with it to attempt to meet those standards.

With the first choice, which is still common, the part-time participant remains a player, dabbler, or dilettante. Following Huizinga's (1955) perspective on play, we can say that leisure of that type lacks necessity, obligation, and utility and will be produced with a disinterestedness that sets it, as an activity, apart from the participants' ordinary, real lives. The second choice, also common and becoming more so, impels part-time participants away from play toward the pursuit of durable benefits. The road to these benefits, however, is characterized by necessity, obligation, seriousness, and commitment, as expressed by regimentation (e.g., rehearsals and practice) and systematization (e.g., schedules and organization), and progresses on to the status of modern amateur for some and professional for others. Godbout (1986) has noted this trend in what he calls the "professionalization of leisure" (also known as regimentation or systematization).

The player of old in sport and music, and quite possibly other fields, was referred to as a "gentleman" (very few were women). But first Huizinga (1955, chap. 12), and then Stone (1971, p. 48), have commented on such players gradual disappearance from sport. Indeed, it is an ongoing process. Barzun (1956, p. 61) points to this transformation in music.

There was a time, furthermore, when players and amateurs (probably differences existed between them even then) were alone in their activities—without professionals to compete against, model themselves after, or simply mingle with. In fact, the early history of many contemporary professions was made up exclusively of amateurs, the only people practicing the professions in their day. In effect, these endeavors were too new, too little in demand, or too underdeveloped to be pursued as livelihoods. In other words, when their fields began, a number of astronomers, archaeologists, teachers, musicians, painters, jugglers, bowlers, soccer players, and so forth earned their living doing something else; clearly, however, they were experts, by the standards of the day, in their respective areas of leisure.

In some fields amateurism was an honourable tradition, and attempts at full-time employment, to say nothing of professionalization, were actually met with derision. At the time, it was considered despicable to make money this way. But, as the two categories of participant began to diverge, it remains to be discovered just how many fields existed in which amateurs could be distinguished from professionals by social class. Whannel (1983, p. 43) notes that, in the nineteenth century, those who played sport for money belonged to the lower class, whereas those who played purely for enjoyment belonged to the upper class. For many years, informal, sometimes even formal, arrangements prevented the different classes of teams and individuals from competing with one another.

As professionals begin to dominate a field pioneered by amateurs, however, a transformation in the meaning of "amateur" seems to have occurred. During this period, old definitions clung tenaciously, merging in common discourse with new ones springing up to describe modern amateurism. From a research standpoint, the result was emergence of the idea of amateur, a term now in everyday life used with annoying imprecision. Entries in *Webster's Unabridged Dictionary* exemplify the problem. Amateurs, for instance, are defined, in one sense, as devotees who love a particular activity; in another sense, however, they are considered superficial participants —dilettantes or dabblers. Dilettantes, on the other hand, are defined, in the first sense, as lovers of the arts and, in the second, as people with discrimination or taste. Consider, also, the logical difficulties posed by yet another sense of "amateur"—that is, the inexperienced person (or player)—and the patent fact that devotees of an activity quite naturally put in much time at it, thereby achieving remarkable competence (i.e., modern amateurs).

When I happened onto the study of amateurism in the early 1970s, sociology was also beset by more or less the same confusion of definitions. My efforts to bring some clarity to the matter, which were based on exploratory research, were discussed briefly on p. 51. This is as much detail about these definitions as needed in this chapter, where I want to avoid digressing further from its central subject: serious leisure.

Hobbyism: Past and Present

Steven Gelber (1999) has written the definitive history of hobbies, which I have used as principal source for this section. The broad trends he observed, based on an examination of British and American sources, apply more generally to industrialized capitalist

Europe and North America from mid-nineteenth century to the end of the 1950s, the point at which he terminates his analysis.

Gelber (1999, p. 1) holds that "industrialism quarantined work from leisure in a way that made employment more worklike and nonwork more problematic. Isolated from each other's moderating influences, work and leisure became increasingly oppositional as they competed for finite hours." Americans, he says, responded in two ways to the threat posed by leisure as potential mischief caused by idle hands. Reformers tried to eliminate or at least restrict access to inappropriate activity, while encouraging people to seek socially approved free-time outlets. Hobbies and other serious leisure pursuits were high on the list of such outlets. In short, "the ideology of the workplace infiltrated the home in the form of productive leisure" (Gelber, 1999, p. 2).

Hobbies were particularly valued, because they bridged especially well the worlds of work and home. And both sexes found them appealing, albeit mostly not the same ones. Some hobbies allowed home-bound women to practice, and therefore understand, worklike activities, whereas other hobbies allowed men to create in the female-dominated house their own businesslike space—the shop in the basement or the garage. Among the various hobbies, two stood out as almost universally approved in these terms: collecting and handicrafts. Still, before approximately 1880, before becoming defined as productive use of free time, these two hobbies, as well as others, were considered "dangerous obsessions."

Gelber (1999, pp. 3-4) notes that, although the forms of collecting and craftwork have changed somewhat during the past 150 years, their meaning has remained the same. Hobbies have been, all along, "a way to confirm the verities of work and the free market inside the home so long as remunerative employment has remained elsewhere" (p. 4).

As for social class both craftwork and collecting appear to be more inclusive of white-collar workers *and* blue-collar producers than they are exclusive of them. Nonetheless, socioeconomic data for these hobbies are presently thin and even thinner back in time, so definitive statements on this question must wait. Meanwhile, Gelber (1999, p. 5) is convinced that hobbies have always transcended class much more readily than they have transcended gender. This squares with my own observations on this question for all serious leisure (Stebbins, 2001a, p. 130).

History of Volunteering

Before presenting this brief history of volunteering, a few words are in order about the resources available for such an exposition. They are, in short, meagre. Lautenschlager (1992, p. iii) notes that her historical account of volunteering in Canada, for example, is the first work of its kind: "Over the years hours and hours of volunteering have been devoted to humanitarian causes, but it still remains to record these efforts on the pages of history" (author's translation). Moreover, her account is limited to formal volunteering, and within that category, she is concerned primarily with *needs volunteering*—helping people solve their personal problems in such areas as health, welfare, and disaster—and *ideological volunteering*—helping promote particular ideals related to women, children, religion, and the like. *Ethnic community volunteering*, for instance, is ignored, though it must have occurred wherever such communities existed. The situation is virtually the same in the United States, where Jones and Herrick (1976, pp. xiii, xvi) report a unique study of formal needs volunteering only, as analysed for the period running from 1929 to 1941.

Volunteering from c.1300 to 1960

Fragnière (1987, pp. 30-31) provides a brief summary of the handful of works on the history of volunteering in general. He writes that, in Europe from the Middle Ages on, volunteering gradually came into its own first as a form of philanthropy expressed in charitable giving to the Roman Catholic Church by people with sufficient money. The Church, which obliged this largesse through its teachings, used these contributions to construct and operate its churches, hospitals, and almshouses. It also engaged lay volunteers with increasing frequency over the years to help serve the clientele of these institutions. In fact, all the great religions, among them Judaism, Buddhism, Islam, and the whole of Christianity, have long recognized and encouraged the materially well off to aid the less fortunate.

Toward the end of the nineteenth century, Western social thought changed, however, drifting toward a concern with rights of humankind, including the right of indigents to aid. They were commonly defined as unfortunate victims of society's evolution, whom more fortunate people had an obligation to help in repayment of their own debt for being spared the same fate. Nevertheless, this sense of obligation waned significantly in the twentieth century, partly because the emerging welfare state made it seem unnecessary and partly because welfare problems were qualified as to complicated for lay attention. At this time the modern nation-state replaced religious and other private-sector authorities to become the primary philanthropic agency in society. And since society was willing to pay people to provide for needs of the poor, needs volunteering professionalized. This pushed to the sidelines altruistic, unpaid helpers, although in the United States during the Great Depression, a shortage of professional social workers forced them to rely frequently on volunteers (Jones and Herrick 1976: chap. 2).

Volunteering from 1960 to 1980

Then more recently, as the welfare system began to erode, volunteers began to reappear, recycled in accordance with contemporary requirements and thus very different from the needs and ideological volunteers of the past. The post-1960s volunteer is best described as a responsible citizen who chooses to work in one or two of the previously mentioned sixteen institutional sectors of modern community life where altruistic help is required. Poverty and health care—the main areas of nineteenth century volunteering—are but two of the sixteen.

This was in fact an era of great governmental expansion in North America, and with this expansion came a multitude of new opportunities for formal volunteering in many of the sectors of community volunteering. The effect of organizational expansion on volunteering during this period is complicated, however. There were undoubtedly many more organizations than previously, but there was also sufficient government funding to pay people to run at least some aspects of a number of them and to pay the costs of implementing some of the services and programs they provided. In this regard, the occasional respondent in the Calgary-Edmonton volunteer study opined that, during the 1970s and 1980s, this government largesse discouraged voluntary action in organizations (Stebbins 1998, p. 20). Still, it can also be argued that many new volunteer roles were created during these years of relative wealth, because organizations had the means to take on certain new projects and services. Occasionally officers were paid or given substantial honoraria, but most served without remuneration, even though their responsibilities were at least as complex and important as those of their remunerated colleagues.

Volunteering after 1980

While it remains to be established whether the amount of volunteering really increased, decreased, or continued at the same level during the second phase of its history, there is no doubt that it has increased dramatically in the third phase. Lautenschlager (1992, pp. 31-32) says the Canadian federal government decided early in the 1980s to start selectively reducing budgets for some of the volunteer programs it supported. At the same time in the United States, President Reagan (in office from 1980 to 1988) was, in this area, taking more draconian measures.

On the most general level, the reductions have inflated sharply the need for volunteers, especially "key volunteers" in leadership positions (Stebbins 1998, pp. 3-5). Why? Because it falls to the latter to fill such posts as president and director, some of which were once funded and therefore once a livelihood or substantial honorarium for incumbents. Additionally, more volunteer help is now needed to raise money to compensate for the shortfall from government, often accomplished nowadays by holding bingos, raffles, or casinos or by conducting fund-raising campaigns. Moreover, toady's volunteer spends more time in meetings seeking new ways to raise money, avoid frivolous expenditures in a bare-bones budget, reduce programs and services to the minimum, and justify to government use of the meagre funds they receive from it. Many interviewees in the Calgary-Edmonton study groaned that the amount of paperwork required in such efforts had now reached extraordinary proportions. Together, the meetings and the paperwork increase the amount of time all volunteers must give to groups and organizations, while leaving just that much less for pursuing other volunteer roles in the community. Consequently, key volunteers must also recruit new members to fill these other roles, though many respondents said such people are becoming increasingly difficult to find. This, then, is one concrete expression in the volunteer world of an emerging personal and collective dependency on the third sector, one indelible stamp of the Information Age (Stebbins, 1998).

Why the reduction in government funding? According to Rifkin (1995) and Aronowitz and Difazio (1994), among others, the world has now entered the early years of the Information Age, gripped by dramatic declines in employment and public sector service and a concomitant rise in the "third sector" and the personal and collective dependency on volunteers. This sector constitutes the home of the nonprofit, voluntary action part of the economy; it stands apart from the sectors of government and for-profit, private industry. The third sector encompasses not only the multitude of charitable organizations and philanthropic foundations, but also the lively world of informal helping.

Here the propensity at all levels of government has been, and seems likely to continue to be, to respond to sharply diminished revenues by cutting or reducing numerous publicly funded health, social, and educational programs and services, with the slack to be taken up by volunteers. While there will surely be some demand for casual volunteering in the expanded third sector, most of the needed volunteering will be of the serious, career variety. This, then, is the political and economic environment in which modern volunteering presently operates in Canada, the United States, and many other industrialized nations.

Motivation in Serious Leisure

The foregoing history of amateurism, hobbyism, and volunteering shows in general terms that, as Gelber observed for craftwork and collecting, there has been considerable variation in the form of activities while their meaning has undergone little change. Thus the following discussion of motives, because they are closely aligned with the meanings of activities, would also appear to be a discussion of historical universals; serious leisure motives observed in the present are the same or very similar to those we would have observed in the past.

And it is a central proposition of serious leisure theory that to understand the meaning of such leisure for those who pursue it is in significant part to understand their motivation for the pursuit. Motives in serious leisure are of two kinds. *Activity motives* relate directly to the central activity; they are the reasons—referred to here as rewards—why it appeals so intensely to those who pursue it. *Social motives* relate indirectly to the central activity; they emerge instead from various social arrangements that spring up around it, which have their own special attraction. Further, as argued in this book, to understand serious leisure motivation is to understand much of the meaning of and motivation for occupational devotion. Finally, one fruitful approach to understanding the motives that lead to serious leisure participation has been to examine them through the eyes of participants who, past studies reveal, see it as a mix of offsetting costs and rewards experienced in the central activity.

Activity Motives: Rewards

Accordingly, most research on serious leisure motivation has used qualitative methods for the direct exploration of particular amateur, hobbyist, and volunteer activities (e.g., Stebbins, 1996a; 1998; Arai and Pedlar, 1997; see Stebbins, 1992, chap. 6 for a summary of his earlier works in this area). This approach has led to discovery of a distinctive set of rewards for each activity examined. In these studies the participant's leisure fulfillment has been found to stem from a constellation of particular rewards gained from the activity, whether playing music, collecting stamps, or teaching crafts to the elderly. Furthermore, these rewards are not only fulfilling in themselves, but also fulfilling as counterweights to the costs encountered in the activity.

That is, every serious leisure activity contains its own pattern of costs—a distinctive combination of tensions, dislikes and disappointments—which each participant confronts in a personal way. For instance, a volunteer board member may not always feel like attending board meetings, occasionally have his or her ideas rejected when there, be asked to perform a disagreeable task from time to time, and still regard this activity as highly fulfilling—as (serious) leisure—because it also offers certain powerful rewards. Put more precisely, then, the drive to gain fulfillment in serious leisure is the drive to experience the rewards of a given leisure activity, such that its costs are seen by participants as more or less insignificant by comparison

That rewards *and* costs exist in serious leisure suggests the profit hypothesis from social exchange theory as a central proposition in a complete explanation of leisure motivation of participants. Homans (1974, p. 31) holds that "the greater the profit [excess of reward over cost] a person receives as a result of his action, the more likely he is to perform the action." This profit is at once the fundamental meaning of the activity for the participant and that person's motivation for engaging in it. It is this motivational sense of the concept of reward that distinguishes it from the idea of durable benefit set out earlier, an idea that emphasizes outcomes rather than antecedent conditions. Nonetheless, the two ideas constitute two sides of the same social psychological coin.

The rewards of a serious leisure pursuit are the more or less routine personal values that attract and hold its enthusiasts. Moreover, several of these values are, at bottom, internalizations of the cultural values considered in chapter 1. Every serious leisure career both frames and is framed by a continuous search for these rewards, a search that takes months, and in some fields years, before participants consistently find deep fulfillment in their amateur, hobbyist, or volunteer role. Ten rewards have so far emerged in the course of the several exploratory studies of amateurs, hobbyists, and career volunteers. As the following list shows, these rewards are predominantly personal.

Personal rewards

1. Personal enrichment (e.g., cherished experiences)
2. Self-actualization, or self-development (i.e., developing skills, abilities, knowledge, acquiring experience)
3. Self-expression (i.e., expressing skills, abilities, knowledge already developed)
4. Self-image (i.e., known to others as a particular kind of serious leisure participant)
5. Self-gratification (i.e., combination of superficial enjoyment and deep fulfillment)
6. Re-creation, or regeneration, of oneself through serious leisure after a day's work
7. Financial return from a serious leisure activity

Social rewards

8. Social attraction (e.g., associating with other serious leisure participants, with clients as a volunteer; participating in the social world of the activity)
9. Group accomplishment (e.g., group effort in accomplishing a serious leisure project; senses of helping, being needed, being altruistic)
10. Contribution to the maintenance and development of the group (e.g., senses of helping, of being needed, of being altruistic in making the contribution)

Although these rewards will be discussed in greater detail in the next chapter, let us consider here how they give substance to certain internalized cultural values. Thus, through particular activities, participants experience the values of achievement and success through the rewards of self-actualization, self-expression, group accomplishment, and contribution to the maintenance and development of the group. The value of activity is felt in the rewards of self-expression and self-gratification, while that of individual personality is felt in the rewards of self-enrichment and self-image. The value of freedom is experienced in all leisure, although even in this sphere, some would-be participants feel constrained to avoid certain activities.

The main types of costs, which exist as counterweights to the rewards, are dislikes, tensions, and disappointments. So far, it has been impossible to develop a general list of costs, similar to that of rewards, since the costs examined tend to be highly specific to each serious leisure activity. Thus, although each serious leisure activity 'studied to date has been found to have its own constellation of costs, those costs are, as interviewees consistently evaluate them, invariably and heavily outweighed in importance by the rewards of the activity (see Stebbins, 2001a, pp. 14-15). The same was found for the professionals interviewed in the studies of amateur-professional magic, football, astronomy, and stand-up comedy.

Social Motives: Social Arrangements

Moreover, certain social arrangements also motivate serious leisure participants, arrangements found in the work of many occupational devotees as well. These include leisure (work) lifestyle and various organizational ties, mainly social networks, small groups, large-scale organizations, and social worlds. Subjective sense of career in the activity constitutes a further incentive to pursue it.

Lifestyle. Dictionary definitions, which tend to portray lifestyle as simply a way of living, are for the most part circular and hence of little use in the present discussion. Social science definitions have advanced well beyond this truism. Thus "a lifestyle is a distinctive set of shared patterns of tangible behavior that is organized around a set of coherent interests or social conditions or both, that is explained and justified by a set of related values, attitudes, and orientations and that, under certain conditions, becomes the basis for a separate, common social identity for its participants" (Stebbins 1997b). Note that this definition refers exclusively to collective lifestyles. This restriction is not to deny the existence of idiosyncratic, highly personal, lifestyles led by recluses, workaholics, people suffering from acute mental disorder, and other loners. Rather the restriction recognizes that, to this point, the study of lifestyles has concentrated almost entirely on shared patterns of tangible behavior, leaving us with little information about individual lifestyles (Veal 1993).

According to the foregoing definition, some lifestyles offer their participants a special social identity. In other words, the participants are members of a category of humankind who recognize themselves and, to some extent, are recognized by the larger community for the distinctive mode of life they lead. Prostitutes, beach habitués, travelling sales people, and the institutionalized elderly are identifiable in many ways, possibly the most visible being their peculiar lifestyles. The same can be said for the enthusiasts pursuing many of the serious leisure activities.

Two essential components of lifestyle are evident in the routine ways participants use time and space to pursue their serious leisure. Leisure lifestyle, then, is about daily, weekly, monthly, or yearly schedules of activities, responsibilities, events, and so on, which routinely take place at given geographic locations. For example, many sports and performing arts groups hold daily or weekly practice sessions. I belong to a group of jazz musicians who jam together weekly. Volunteers constituting the executive of a community organization often meet monthly, while the organization as a whole schedules an annual general meeting for all members.

To meet with each other, whether as friends, teammates, or colleagues, requires that most participants leave home or work to go to another part of the community or, in some instances, another part of the region, nation, even the planet. So, often, the pursuit of serious leisure helps enthusiasts become familiar with, for example, buildings and geographic points seldom if ever encountered while doing everyday domestic and occupational routines. Furthermore, the routes by which they reach these places make up another facet of the particular spatial structuring that goes with a given activity. Because people participate in it, they must, to meet with other participants, pass through neighborhoods, deal with traffic patterns, observe land use arrangements, and the like they would not likely have encountered otherwise.

Thus an interesting lifestyle awaits anyone who routinely pursues a serious leisure career in, say, amateur theater, volunteer work with the mentally handicapped, the hobby of model railroading, or that of mountain climbing. Because it gives temporal structure and spatial variety to life, this leisure lifestyle has its own appeal; it becomes in itself a motive for participation in the activity.

Organizational Ties. Whether as incentives for joining a leisure organization or as incentives for remaining in one, I have discussed elsewhere (Stebbins, 2002a, pp. 2-4) several meanings that, together, constitute a powerful force leading people to establish such organizations, or if already established, to get involved with them or continue their membership there. Put more broadly, the very fact that leisure organizations exist and exist in great numbers contributes significantly to the scientific explanation of why people go in for collective leisure activities.

Note that leisure organizations are being treated of here as forms of social organization, as that term is used in sociology and anthropology. What is social organization? Guy Rocher defines it as "the total arrangement of all the elements which serve to structure social action into a whole, which has an image or a particular form which is different from its constituent parts and also different from other possible arrangements" (Rocher, 1972, p. 149). In leisure, as in many other areas of life, action is structured, or organized, in small groups (including dyads and triads), social networks, and grassroots organizations as well as in larger complex organizations and still more broadly, in social worlds, and social movements. Each structures the social behavior of its members in particular ways, some of those ways being unique to that kind of organization.

Still, Rocher's definition fails to consider a central aspect of social organizational life: individual interests also structure organizations of every sort, including instituting them in the first place. Thus we may say about leisure organizations, as with other kinds, that participation in them amounts to a two-way street of influence from individual to collectivity and collectivity to individual.

What attracts people to organizations? A particular organization is important to its members, because through it, they find a sense of belonging to a *distinctive* and *identifiable* part of the larger human world in which they live. Be that organization a friendship, poker club, political party, or international network of ham radio operators, each member feels the distinctiveness that comes from being included in it while all nonmembers are excluded from it. Moreover, the organization in question can be identified and described; it has a *social reality* of its own for both members and outsiders who are aware of it (Borgatta, 1981). It is but a short step from the senses of distinctiveness and social reality of the organization to acquiring both a *social and a personal identity* related to it. A member's identity is social when other people (members and nonmembers) recognize that person as member, as Mary's friend, as participant in the Friday night poker bash, and so on. This identity becomes personal when members present themselves to others as belonging to this or that political party or using ham radio to enjoy some international conversation. Further, all organizations offer some sort of *power and control* to their members. Finally, they help shape personal lifestyles, as they organize some of their members' *time* according to daily, weekly, monthly, or yearly schedules and as they help determine some of the *spatial movement* of their members.

The leisure organizations that bear on occupational devotion are small groups, social networks, volunteer organizations, and social worlds (conceived of here as a form of social organization). Personal interest in particular free-time activities, individuated patterns of leisure lifestyle, and intensive participation in related small groups and social networks, together constitute a substantial explanation of leisure motivation. In trying to pursue a particular leisure interest, the individual soon finds that time and space have become structured in certain ways, which includes routine, if not regular, interaction with certain people in that person's groups and networks. Put otherwise, tangible patterns of behavior emerge, which are appealing in part because they are social. The same holds for volunteer organizations and social worlds.

Volunteer organizations, as the term indicates, offer a leisure outlet for volunteers, some of it casual, some of it of the career variety. There are organizations like religious establishments, seniors centers, and political parties that engage copious numbers of both types, in contrast to other organizations like hospitals, primary schools, and the Peace Corps that rely almost exclusively on career volunteers. Finally, some volunteer organizations need, for the most part, only casual help; they include community food banks, the Salvation Army, and groups whose mission is to provide transportation for the elderly. Amateurs and hobbyists rarely, if ever, form volunteer organizations, although polymorphic structures in these two types of leisure commonly include volunteer organizations at the national or international level. They set guidelines and offer important services for constituent units functioning locally.

Research has also revealed that, in themselves, serious leisure social worlds, when recognized as such, become attractive formations (Stebbins, 1999, p. 267), though they appear to inspire people more to stay in them than to join them in the first place. Usually, it takes time to learn about the social world of, say, darts or volunteering for the Scouts or Guides, something that really only effectively occurs once inside that world. Nevertheless, I found that belonging to and participating in the social worlds of theater, entertainment magic, stand-up comedy, and classical music were heady experiences for many of the amateurs I interviewed. For them, membership and participation constituted two additional powerful reasons for pursuing their art, albeit two social reasons. This is true, in part, because belonging to such a world helps socially locate individual artists in mass urban society as well as helps personalize to some extent their involvement there. Today's serious leisure social world is, in general, significantly less impersonal than either the modern mass or the postmodern "tribe" (Maffesoli, 1996). Moreover, serious leisure activities generate their own attractive lifestyles, which are associated with particular social worlds.

In fact, nearly every serious leisure activity is anchored in a vibrant social world endowed with the capacity—once recognized— to attract and hold a large proportion of its participants. Although the activity itself is exciting, the excitement it generates is also greatly enhanced by the presence of networks of like-minded regulars and insiders, important strangers, local and national organizations, spaces for pursuing the activity, and tourists who visit from time to time— the audiences, spectators admirers, onlookers, and others. Magazines, newsletters, courses, lectures, workshops, and similar channels of information make up another prominent part of the typical serious leisure enthusiast's social world.

Career. The idea of a subjective career refers to the practitioner's recognition and interpretation of the events—past, present, and future—associated with his or her work or leisure role (Stebbins, 1970a). Especially important in any analysis of the subjective side of a career is the practitioners' interpretation of the turning points already encountered or expected. It is from a description of their subjective careers that we learn how amateurs and professionals have determined continuity in their work and leisure lives - how they see themselves as progressing or declining.

Exploratory research on careers in serious leisure has so far proceeded from a broad, rather loose definition: a leisure career is the typical course, or passage, of a type of amateur, hobbyist, or volunteer that carries the person into and through a leisure role and possibly into and through a work role. The essence of any career, whether in work, leisure, or elsewhere, lies in the temporal continuity of the activities associated with it. Moreover, we are accustomed to thinking of this continuity as one of accumulating rewards and prestige, as progress along these lines from some starting point, even though continuity may also include career retrogression. Serious leisure careers have been empirically examined in my own research and that of Baldwin and Norris (1999).

The essence of career lies in the temporal continuity of the activities associated with it. It is common to think of this continuity as one of accumulating rewards and prestige, as progress along these lines from some starting point. But continuity may also include career retrogression. In the worlds of sport and entertainment, for instance, athletes and artists may reach performance peaks early on, after which the prestige and rewards diminish as the limelight shifts to younger, sometimes more capable practitioners.

Career continuity may occur predominantly within, between, or outside organizations. Careers in organizations such as a community orchestra or hobbyist association only rarely involve the challenge of the "bureaucratic crawl," to use the imagery of C. Wright Mills. In other words, little or no hierarchy exists for them to climb. Nevertheless, the amateur or hobbyist still gains a profound sense of continuity, and hence career, from his or her more or less steady development as a skilled, experienced, and knowledgeable participant in a particular form of serious leisure and from the deepening sense of fulfillment that accompanies this kind of personal growth. Some volunteer careers are intraorganizational as well.

Still, many amateurs and volunteers as well as some hobbyists have careers that bridge two or more organizations. For them, career continuity stems from their growing reputations as skilled, knowledgeable practitioners and, based on this image, from finding increasingly better leisure opportunities available through various outlets (as in different teams, orchestras, organizations, tournaments, exhibitions, journals, conferences, contests, shows, and the like). Meanwhile, still other amateurs and hobbyists, who pursue noncollective lines of leisure (e.g., tennis, painting, clowning, golf, entertainment magic), are free of even this marginal affiliation with an organization. The extraorganizational career of the informal volunteer, the forever willing and sometimes highly skilled and knowledgeable helper of friends, relatives, and neighbors is of this third type.

Serious Leisure in Society and Culture

Gelber affirmed earlier that, historically, hobbies have been largely classless, and that they have been sensitive to gender only in the kinds of activities taken up (e.g., men make furniture, women make quilts). Moreover, I have argued elsewhere that these patterns hold for all contemporary serious leisure (Stebbins, 2001a, p. 112), including differentiation at times by class and gender according to kinds of activities pursued. For example, some working-class men prefer motorcross, while some middle-class men and a smaller number of middle-class women go in for fly-fishing for trout. Unfortunately, the age and racial bases of serious leisure, among other possible demographic correlates, have not been widely explored; thus no empirical grounds exist presently for the kind of observations being made in this paragraph.

From a cultural standpoint, the enthusiast's approach to serious leisure clearly resembles in several respects the approach to work referred to earlier as the modern work ethic: hard work is intrinsically virtuous and worthy of reward. This likeness is most evident in the first three distinctive qualities of serious leisure: the need to persevere, the appeal of a (leisure) career, and the requirement of making a personal effort in pursuing the activity. These similarities raise the intriguing question of which came first, these three qualities of serious leisure or the Protestant ethic as precursor of the present-day work ethic? We will probably never know fully the answer to this question, but allow me one provocative observation: amateurs, hobbyists, and volunteers have generally preceded their commercial and professional counterparts. Perhaps devoted work and serious leisure have always had a greater reciprocal influence than scholars in this area have realized.

Discussion in this chapter of serious leisure motivation—rewards, costs, social arrangements—has been necessarily abstract. Moreover, rather little has been said here about work, since the entire chapter was needed to set out the basic leisure framework for analyzing of occupational devotion. We return to work in the next chapter, however, where in much greater detail, occupational devotion will be explained using the serious leisure motivational framework just set out.

5

Erasing the Line between Work and Leisure

In the preceding chapter we examined in broad terms the various ways in which the line between devotee work and serious leisure is erased. What remains to be accomplished in this chapter is to show more concretely just how thin this line actually is. As mentioned, however, being paid is a condition of work that ensures this line will never be completely effaced.

Leisure Prefigures Work

Although exceptions exist, which will also be duly considered in this chapter, a large majority of today's devotee occupations actually owe their existence in one way or another to one or more serious leisure precursors. The histories of amateurism, hobbyism, and volunteerism presented in chapter 4 made this point in a most general way. Let us now look more closely at the details.

Amateurs Become Professionals

I observed earlier that every professional field in art, science, sport, and entertainment made its debut with a gang of enthusiastic amateurs who pioneered the way. Thus in all these areas the love for the core activity got its start in free time. But for some of these amateurs, their free time was too limited. It would be nice, they reasoned, were they able to engage full-time in such absorbing, fulfilling, and rewarding undertakings. So once society's need for the activity caught up with the desire of some of its practitioners to pursue it at length, the emergence of the professional wing was all but ensured.

But if amateurs always have professional counterparts, the reverse, at first glance, might appear to be impossible. In other words, do professionals always have amateur counterparts? To begin, let us note that client-centered professionals are authenticated by formal licensing procedures based on specialized training, which among other things, are meant to generate for their clients the impression that they are receiving competent and certified advice and treatment. Furthermore, each profession exercises monopolistic control over who receives this training, as offered in a set of occupations that form around problematic areas of life where uncertainty is too acute to permit unfettered, free enterprise to supply the remedy. We need control in these areas, which we have granted in substantial degree to the client-centered professions. Not so, however, with the public-centered professions. They form instead in various expressive areas of life, where there is no acute uncertainty and where, as a result, no one has acquired the right of control, including even the professions themselves.

Still, client-centered professionals must be trained, and here is where amateurs (and, as noted below, sometimes volunteers) enter the picture. In particular, it is plausible to describe these trainees as "preprofessional amateurs" (Stebbins, 1979, p. 36), who as they take courses, engage in practical work, and learn just how fulfilling their future profession can be, develop a substantial devotion to it. The practical work gives them the opportunity to do at least some of the core tasks done by their professional counterparts. All this occurs in an atmosphere that is essentially one of serious leisure, in that students can and do at times quit these training programs, giving substance to their basically noncoercive nature.

Hobbyists become Crafts/Small Business People

Since today's trades invariably require formal schooling, many of the same recruitment and training arrangements prevail here as in the client-centered professions. What we will call "preapprentice" student hobbyists discover in their own courses and applied work a set of core tasks quite capable of engendering fulfillment and occupational devotion. Like their professional counterparts, it is rare that these hobbyists will have had as hobbyists any significant prior contact with their chosen trade. With both groups, the trade or profession for which the student is training is evaluated from an external vantage point by that person. From here it appears to offer interesting, fulfilling work as well as a decent living. So why not try it (assuming the usual financial and academic admission requirements can be met)?

People going into one of the many of the small businesses have career patterns similar to those who become enamored of one of the public-centered professions. That is, occupational devotees in small business often get started as pure hobbyists, the family farm being an exception to this observation. Thus, commercial genealogists, who seem to develop a taste for their core activity through earlier historical work on their own families, enter the business world from a pure hobbyist background, as do those in the artistic crafts, repair and restoration, and dealing in collectibles.

Volunteers become Organizational Workers

Among the organizational volunteers are those who use their altruistic role to explore for work in a particular segment of the job market. Sometimes these "marginal volunteers" (Stebbins, 2001d, pp. 4-6) hope to find employment by this route, accomplished by gaining experience that will better their chances of getting work in that field or a related one. Sometimes they simply want to explore the nature of work there, and sometimes they believe that volunteer experience will look good on their resume. This less-than-pure volunteering is common practice these days, especially in the age bracket fifteen to twenty-four (Statistics Canada, 2001, p. 37). Yet, even when people are operating under pressure and obligation to find some sort of work and who "volunteer" their services as part of their search for such work, there are those who manage to find an occupation worthy of their devotion.

On the other hand, pure organizational volunteers—those who serve primarily for the fulfillment derived from executing attractive core tasks—may be hired to fill a remunerative post in their organization that generates occupational devotion. One such post is volunteer coordinator; it includes recruiting volunteers and matching them according to their capabilities and interests with the volunteer needs of the organization. And some pure organizational volunteers learn at close range about the fulfilling aspects of certain kinds of professional work carried out in their organization, giving them impetus to seek the training they need for this new career. A number of social workers, registered nurses, and recreational specialists got started this way.

Rewards

In the preceding chapter we set out, in rather abstract terms, the activity and social motives framework, defining it in parallel as the set of rewards serious leisure participants derive from their free time efforts. The aim of this section is to put some empirical meat on these theoretical bones, by showing how both these leisure participants and their allied occupational devotees are motivated and rewarded by nearly identical interests. Research by Juniu, Tedrick, and Boyd (1996) and my own studies of amateurs and professionals (reviewed in Stebbins, 1992) provide a reasonable amount of empirical support for the observations made in this section.

The first reward mentioned was personal enrichment, which has to do with the cherished, occasionally thrilling, experiences that come from time to time with doing the core activity. So, winning a championship in a sport is enriching for both professionals and amateurs, as is working with autistic children for both volunteers and child psychologists. The antique dealer is as thrilled to see a beautifully crafted and maintained period chair or table as the collector who just might buy it. The personal enriching experiences of devotees and serious leisure participants alike are tucked away in memory, to provide a vivid chronology of involvement in that line of work or leisure.

The reward of self-actualization, or self-development—the acquisition of substantial skill, knowledge, and experience—is by this point in this book self-evident. This reward, when considered on the theoretical level, is one of the six defining criteria of occupational devotion and one of the six defining characteristics of serious leisure. It is at the very center of self-fulfillment in all work and leisure where it is possible to experience this process. The fact is that we find it hugely rewarding to watch ourselves improve in complex endeavors, endeavors respected by our reference groups and valued in some important way by society.

Self-expression, which includes expression of the acquired skills, knowledge, and experience as well as expression of our inherited abilities, is likewise found in all serious leisure and devotee work. It is rewarding to be able to apply what we have acquired: to play well the violin, to gather useful data by telescope, to make attractive jewelry as a hobby or a small business. Whether amateur or professional, writers get a significant lift from having their books published, as do athletes at both levels when they win championships.

Where it occurs psychological flow is part of this self-expression, especially its components of sense of competence and sense of control. This reward, along with those of self-actualization and self-enrichment, operationalize most directly the idea of self-fulfilment in work and leisure. All research on serious leisure that has looked into the matter has reached this same conclusion (Stebbins, 2001a, p. 14).

Serious leisure participants and occupational devotees alike are proud of what they do, and generalizing from research on the former, they seldom hesitate to talk about it to anyone who will listen. But having a positive self-image from involvement in substantial leisure or work fails to generate the charge of excitement and fulfillment that comes with actual execution of the core activity. True, it is nice to be known by others as, for example, a stamp collector or an antique dealer, and even nicer to be seen in their eyes as a good or very good collector or dealer. Yet neither of these images is usually as exciting as finding a rare stamp in good condition or assessing the beauty and quality of a fine piece of old furniture.

Self-gratification, the personal reward that combines superficial enjoyment and deep fulfillment, speaks to the hedonic side of our motivation to pursue serious leisure or devotee work. That is, it is sometimes just plain fun to play the violin, fly an airplane, or make a quilt, as we experience this reward quite separately from the other rewards of serious leisure and devotee work. Self-gratification is the fun side of devotee work and serious leisure, and many a serious leisure interviewee described the matter exactly in these terms. To some extent this reward is like self-expression, and includes, where possible, the feeling of psychological flow, as enabled by senses of competence and control as well as by clarity of goals and immediate feedback on execution of the activity. Still, self-expression is broader than self-gratification, primarily because, in the first, the fun may be diluted. We see this when challenges are met, but doing so has its unpleasant moments (e.g., managing stage fright in a performing art, laying stone on a hot and humid day, "playing hurt" in sport).

The reward of re-creation, or regeneration, of oneself through serious leisure after a session of work, though clearly important for people taking their leisure, nevertheless falls outside the scope of this book. For this reason it will not be considered further. As for the reward of financial return, a minor reward in all serious leisure, it is obviously of some importance in devotee work. We examine the "money orientation" in the next chapter.

Social attraction, as a reward in serious leisure and devotee work, refers to the pleasant character of the social relations engaged in as an essential part of the core activity. Examples include interesting and attractive interpersonal exchanges among members of a surgery team, a jazz quartet, or a group of lawyers working together on a case, as these people go about their work or leisure. Interchanges that professionals and volunteers have with some of their clients can be of this nature. The concept of social attraction also refers to the respect, mutual liking, and understanding felt among members of a musical group, sport team, or small business. Client-professional relations, including those in the various consulting and counseling fields, often have this same quality. In other words, this reward is significantly more fulfilling than the "social life" mentioned in chapter 1 that emerges as extracurricular leisure snatched in the interstices of work and periods of free time outside it.

Group accomplishment appears as a reward in work and leisure requiring a collective effort to accomplish a certain goal. Volunteers serving in such settings speak of their sense of helping, of being needed, of acting altruistically as part of the collaborative effort. Meanwhile, in the other serious leisure fields and in the different devotee occupations, group accomplishment includes the feeling of being needed but also that of being an important link in the chain or set of tasks that leads to group accomplishment. So this reward is experienced in such successful contributions to team effort as winning a game, performing well a play, running a profitable small business, and generating a workable town plan. To be clear the individualistic reward of working with autistic children is different from the collectivist reward gained from carrying out a successful and complicated surgery.

The final reward—contribution to the maintenance and development of the group—again emphasizes the senses of helping, being needed, and being altruistic in making this contribution. Volunteer contributions that help advance ethnic group interests, interests of the local gay community, or interests of a neighborhood exemplify this reward on the serious leisure side. Social workers and health care professionals working to better the lot of the local poor offer an example on the devotee level. Indeed, routine work in any successful, multiple-employee small business is capable of generating this reward, as workers in devotee and non-devotee roles alike gain a profound sense of helping keep the enterprise afloat and moving forward. In fact, this same feeling can even be found among the employees in mid- and large-sized corporations who still identify with their employers (even if many no longer do this).

Since we are speaking here of motivation, costs though they certainly exist and are to be reckoned with in devotee work, are nonetheless beside the point. In other words, devotee occupations are, on balance, highly rewarding despite their occasional costs. Therefore, failure to dwell in this chapter on costs should not be taken as a sign that none exists. Indeed, they can mount to a burden so great that the devotee job is no longer fulfilling. A dramatic example of this occurred in France where world-renowned chef Bernard Loiseau is believed by some to have committed suicide in reaction to a negative review of his restaurant (*Economist*. 2003b, p. 80). The prestigious restaurant guide *GaultMillau* reduced the restaurant's standing to two from three stars (the highest rating). And the *Economist* (2003a, p. 73) reports in an article on the high cost of medical insurance in the United States that there is growing anecdotal evidence that, in states where these costs are very high, doctors are refusing to practice. But comments by Canadian professional football player Steve Anderson sum well the relationship of rewards to costs for most occupational devotees. "Sometimes playing football is a real bitch, hard and frustrating. . . . It can drive you crazy. So you gotta love it to play it. But if you love it, you stay at it, and keep working, things will turn around for you" (Johnson, 2002, p. F1).

Social Arrangements

Various social arrangements further motivate both serious leisure participants and occupational devotees. These include leisure and work lifestyles as well as various organizational ties, of which the main ones for the purposes of this book are social networks, small groups, large-scale organizations, and social worlds. A person's subjective sense of his career in the core activity serves as yet another prominent incentive to stay involved there.

Lifestyle

Work lifestyle is different from leisure lifestyle, with each complementing the other. That much is obvious. The main point, however, is that serious leisure research has found leisure lifestyle to be a powerful motive for engaging in a particular leisure activity. Moreover, the same would seem to hold for devotee work. But bear in mind during our discussion of lifestyle that not all use of personal time is accounted for by work and leisure. That is, leisure occurs in free time, work in work time (including household work), while nonwork obligations are met in a third zone of everyday living. Bodily maintenance activities are part of this zone (e.g., bathing, hair care, brushing teeth), as is routine exercise for people who define it as other than leisure. And to the extent there is a sense of coercion about them, routine obligations to relatives, neighbors, and community fall here as well.

This section, however, is concerned not with nonwork obligations but with the nature of lifestyles in the other two zones that spring up around serious leisure and devotee work. The practices and their distribution over the days and weeks comprising a person's work or leisure lifestyle come, in regard to serious leisure and devotee work, to be fondly regarded. These are the spaces in life where the enthusiast pursues personally fulfilling activities, where life is often highly exciting, where time flies, and so forth. Figuratively put for occupational devotees, "thank-God-it's-Friday" and "blue Monday" are not part of the vocabulary they use to describe work, for their work lifestyles are largely filled with pleasant memories and anticipations. They have no need for bumper stickers like "a bad day diving is better than a good day at work."

Consequently, a work lifestyle of this kind is, upon retirement, likely to be sorely missed. Indeed, one of the attractive features of serious leisure is that some of its lifestyles can provide a decent substitute for what the retired devotee left behind. The same is true for some of the unemployed, even though many of them are often overwhelmed by the act of being thrown out of work, suffering from depression and lethargy to the extent that pursuing leisure of any kind becomes next to impossible (Kay, 1990, p. 415). Part of the problem, it seems, is that they feel useless and pressured by social convention to search unceasingly for work, a frame of mind that virtually alienates them from true leisure. That is, they are too demoralized to engage in leisure, a purposive activity designed to achieve a particular end. Meanwhile, sitting around idle and bored, even though it occurs in free time, is no more leisure than it is work.

Social Networks

Many kinds of devotee work and serious leisure are organized, among other ways, along the lines of various social networks. The definition of social network that best fits the present discussion is Elizabeth Bott's (1957, p. 59). Her definition is simple: a social network is "a set of social relationships for which there is no common boundary." In the strict sense of the word, a network is not a structure, since it has no shared boundaries (boundaries recognized by everyone in the social network) and no commonly recognized hierarchy or central coordinating agency. Nevertheless, interconnections exist between others in the network, in that some members are directly in touch with each other while others are not. Thus it is also true of networks that their mesh may be "closely-knit" (many members having direct contact) or "loosely-knit" (few members having direct contact) (Barnes, 1954; Bott, 1957, p. 59). As for their size, many social networks are no larger than most small groups, even though some can be so large and extensive that they span regional or national boundaries.

Over the years, social networks have been analyzed from two basic approaches. One is ego-centered, the view of the network of a particular individual who is part of it. The other is holistic; here the component relationships are seen as the sum of every individual's personal network. Both approaches help explain participation in serious leisure and devotee work. The first, which is the more common in network analyses in leisure studies, examines the structure of social interaction, starting with the relationships one person maintains with others in that person's network, defined as "points," and then tracing those relationships as "lines" connecting the points.

As individuals pursue their leisure or work interests, they develop networks of contacts (friends and acquaintances) related in one way or another to these interests. As a person develops more such interests, the number of networks grows accordingly, bearing in mind that members of some of these will nevertheless sometimes overlap. In trying to pursue a particular interest, the individual soon finds that time and space have become structured in certain ways, which include routine, if not regular, interaction with certain people in that person's networks. Put otherwise, tangible patterns of behavior emerge, which are appealing, in significant part because they are social. Moreover, social networks are important for generating work or leisure opportunities (and sometimes both) and motivating people to take advantage of them. For instance, a few members of John's dog breeding network—they might be suppliers, veterinarians, or other breeders—are also members of his golf network—who might be suppliers, course personnel, or other golfers. Knowing people's work and leisure networks helps explain how they socially organize their time in these spheres of life.

Small Groups

The small group, a concept that includes dyads and triads, generates its own idioculture, or distinctive set of shared ideas that emerge with reference to it (Fine, 1979). Idioculture is local culture, developed within and as an expression of an actual small group. It consists of a system of knowledge, beliefs, behaviors, and customs peculiar to that collectivity. Members use this system when interacting with one another, expecting that they will be understood by other members.

Participation in these groups brings distinctive benefits of its own, experienced in the form of two of the social rewards mentioned earlier: social attraction and group accomplishment. The key point to be made here is that serious leisure research has demonstrated the existence of these benefits for the leisure domain, suggesting as well that such rewarding participation can also be found in devotee occupations. Thus not to be overlooked in these occupations as attractions of the core activity are the highly fruitful and personally attractive dyadic arrangements so common among musicians, lawyers, athletes, scientists, and business people, to mention a few.

Large-Scale Organizations

It may come as a surprise to find in this book a discussion of large-scale organizations, when in various places throughout, I have maintained that occupational devotion cannot take root in any, but at most, lightly bureaucratized arrangements. Moreover, serious leisure participants generally operate outside medium and large bureaucracies, though at times they rely on them for certain services and products (e.g., park services that supply sports facilities, companies that sell equipment, universities that offer continuing education courses). The principal and widespread exception to this rule comes from the many volunteers who serve in volunteer organizations. Volunteer organizations are distinguished by their reliance on paid staff, and by the fact that they are established to facilitate work for a cause or provision of a service rather than pursuit of a pastime. They nonetheless depend significantly on volunteer help to reach their goals. Indeed, volunteers may far outnumber paid staff in these organizations, although the opposite is true for such volunteer organizations as hospitals and universities.

Turning now to occupational devotees, they sometimes find work in such entities as, for example, volunteer coordinators or as professionals working in a specialized capacity (e.g., expert in recreation, sports medicine, or library science). But how, then, do these devotees, and others employed in similar circumstances, succeed in meeting Criterion 4 (chap. 1), in gaining reasonable control over amount and disposition of time put into their work, so that they, too, can enjoy the work life of an occupational devotee? As near as I can tell they usually fail to do this. True, some do manage to survive in large bureaucracies, among them the volunteer coordinator, who is, however, basically marginal to the structure of his organization, because this person works primarily with people who are not even members of it. This person's function is to relate to a set of volunteers who themselves are marginal to the organization's bureaucracy, as are hospital volunteers to central hospital administration and Olympic games volunteers to the national Olympic association. Provided the volunteer corps is working well, its coordinator will most probably be left alone to do what must be done to maintain this happy state.

As for organizational professionals, both MacDonald (1995, pp. 61-63), based on his review of the literature, and Wallace (1995b), based on her research on lawyers, argue that the work of such professionals usually meets what we have been referring to as the six defining criteria. Their conclusions challenge the proletarianization hypothesis that professional work is also subject to the forces of deskilling. Nevertheless, both authors fail to address themselves to the modern organizational tendency to squeeze every once of work possible from its employees, making a lie of Criterion 4. "At cutting-edge corporations, which emphasize commitment, initiative, and flexibility, the time demands are often the greatest" (Schor, 1991, p. 19). Schor says further that a combination of retrenchment, economic competition, and innovative business management has, for high-powered employees, led to a substantial raise in number of working hours. Data collected in September 2002 from a random sample of mid- and large-sized corporate employees in North America reveal that this tendency is still very much alive (Towers Perrin, 2003). Additional evidence for it comes from a survey of practicing physicians, which found that 50 percent of the sample traced hospital errors to stress, fatigue, and overwork of health professionals (Blendon, et al, 2002). Such pressure-cooker environments are inimical to occupational devotion, which is why present-day bureaucratic organizations are only rarely able to retain workers inspired by it.

Consultants, however, can avoid such treatment. To the extent that the bureaucratic sweatshop is now giving way to the "neo-entrepreneurial workplace," as Leicht and Fennel (2001) refer to it, consultants and other employees viewed in this new paradigm as "independent contractors" will have significant control over disposition of their time. Altogether, the future of occupational devotion appears dimmest in highly bureaucratized settings.

Social World

Having defined and described in sufficient detail in the preceding chapter the idea of social world, what remains to be done is to present some examples of it in devotee work. We will consider an example from each of the four occupational areas in which devotee work is routinely found, the examples chosen being ones with which, over the years, I have gained some familiarity.

The social world of the professional, classical music orchestra musician is most complicated. At the center of this social world is the orchestra in which this person plays; this is where much of, if not all, the core devotee activity of making music takes place. The orchestra includes all musical colleagues employed there as well as its regular directors. Moreover, since some orchestra musicians teach their instrument or play in other musical groups (many do both), their social world expands to include the people they work with in these capacities. And North American professionals are very likely members of the American Federation of Musicians of the United

States and Canada, while many also belong to an organization that promotes their particular musical instrument (e.g., International Society of Bassists, National Flute Association). Finally, these musicians usually have an extensive network of contacts, used variously for recruiting students, obtaining extra-orchestral work, finding additional players for their section in the orchestra, and the like. Some are also part-time employees in local schools of music.

Among the typical strangers in the professional classical music world, we find such intermediaries as music store personnel, instrument repair experts, and equipment suppliers (e.g., reeds, rosin, mutes, strings). Its tourists comprise the audience at each concert presented by the orchestra and the people who listen to its recordings. Regulars and insiders are the orchestra's musicians themselves, differentiated in ways described earlier according to their level of commitment, enthusiasm, and involvement in their craft.

The social world of the career counsellor is in many ways simpler than that of the orchestra musician. The office where counselling takes place and individual cases are studied constitutes the center of each counsellor's social world. This is where this devotee pursues the attractive core tasks of his occupation. The career counsellor's world expands from here to include local colleagues, especially those who are partners in the same counselling firm, but also professional colleagues wherever they work. Many of these people will be members of the relevant professional associations such as the American Psychological Association and the National Career Development Association. Some career counsellors have ties with various work organizations, where they give the occasional seminar and workshop on their speciality. Office staff and relationships established with nearby institutions of higher education help round out this social world.

The strangers in career counselling include publishers of psychological tests, professional books, and computer software enabling efficient filing and analyses of individual cases. The counsellor's clients and seminar participants constitute the main tourists in this social world. And the counsellors themselves make up the corps of regulars and insiders in their profession, as differentiated locally according to the criteria just set out for orchestra musicians.

The social world of framing carpenters employed with a house building company will serve as our example for the skilled trades.

Unlike the previous two occupations their work site is constantly changing, as each house is framed. So their social world consists most immediately of housing sites in general, the job site foreman, and the other carpenters who work for the company, only some of whom are assigned to a given site. Additionally, most framing carpenters are members of the United Brotherhood of Carpenters and Joiners of America.

The principal intermediaries are the stores that sell carpenter's tools and supplies and the clothing they need for construction work out of doors. The tourists in this occupation are limited to the company that employs the carpenters, which takes an interest in the quality of work they do, and the governmental inspectors who are mandated to ensure compliance with the local building code. Insiders are differentiated from regulars primarily by the high degree of care and enthusiasm with which they carry out their work.

The social world of small business is exemplified here by the family farm specializing in vegetable farming. It is centered on the farm itself, members of the family who own it and do most if not all the work there, and any hired hands. Other farm families in the neighborhood constitute another important part of this social world. Many farmers are also members of their state's Farm Bureau, which is part of the American Farm Bureau Federation.

Farmers depend on a notable range of strangers, including equipment dealers, those who sell supplies (e.g., seed, gasoline, fertilizer), crop insurance companies, and pesticide services. There may also be need for a watering or irrigation service. Tourists in the world of the family farm are the wholesalers and retailers who buy what is produced on it. Finally, the insider-regular distinction is difficult to apply in this small business, since at least traditionally, family members have usually enacted separate but complementary roles (e.g., he plows the fields, she looks after the accounting). If there is any differentiation here, it is along the dimensions of enthusiasm and dedication shown by each toward his core tasks.

Career

It was noted in chapter 4 that every serious leisure career both frames and is framed by a continuous search for the distinctive rewards of the activity, a search that takes months, and in some fields years, before participants consistently find deep fulfillment in their amateur, hobbyist, or volunteer role. Precisely the same observation can be made about careers in the devotee occupations. In other words, pursuing a career in a serious leisure activity or a devotee occupation is yet another way in which the line separating work and leisure becomes substantially blurred.

We saw how this occurs in serious leisure, so it is now time to see how it occurs in occupational devotion. First of all, there is certainly a sense of subjective career in a given line of devotee work, as those in it meet and interpret the various contingencies and turning points, particularly as these key events relate to the core activity. For instance, a commercial ceramicist might develop an attractive new jewelry design that turns out to be a big seller, or a construction worker works to meet the demanding requirements of master electrician. Both are turning points. Contingencies are also encountered, such as a chemist's serendipitous finding in her laboratory or a small businessman's chance discovery of ideally located commercial space with low rent and favorable tenant conditions.

Research in serious leisure shows that participants who stick with their activities eventually pass through four, possibly five career stages: beginning, development, establishment, maintenance, and decline. The boundaries separating these stages are imprecise, however, for as the condition of continuity suggests, the participant passes largely imperceptibly from one to the next. The beginning lasts as long as is necessary for interest in the activity to take root. Development begins when the interest has taken root and its pursuit becomes more or less routine and systematic. Serious leisure participants advance to the establishment stage once they have moved beyond the requirement of having to learn the basics of their activity. During the maintenance stage, the leisure career is in full bloom; here participants are now able to enjoy to the fullest their pursuit of it, the uncertainties of getting established having, for the most part, been put behind them. By no means do all serious leisure participants face decline. In fact, some never quit. But for those who do face decline, it often results from deteriorating mental or physical skills. A more detailed description of the career framework and its five stages is available elsewhere (Stebbins, 1992, chap. 5; on career in hobbies see Stebbins, 1996a).

Occupational devotees entering their work career after a period of pure amateurism or hobbyism, do so at the establishment stage, whereas those who entering from a preprofessional or "preapprentice" stage do this at the development stage. But whether serious leisure or devotee work, the process is much the same: over the years the individual acquires a combination of skill, knowledge, and experience befitting that person's chosen line of work or leisure, which offers variety and ample opportunity for creativity or innovation. Continuity is felt as these acquisitions mount, as is a sense of career, of getting better and more experienced at one's passion. And with this comes a growing feeling of deep fulfillment. Or, as we put it at the beginning of this section, a devotee's career both frames and is framed by an ongoing search for several of the ten rewards. Career is thus a powerful motivational force in both serious leisure and devotee work.

Talk of career raises a question that has not, to my knowledge, been addressed in either the work or the leisure studies literature: when, if ever, do occupational devotees and serious leisure enthusiasts reach a point where they have had enough of their core activity? The likely impression gained from reading the foregoing is that such a point is never reached, at least never reached psychologically. Injury, extraneous circumstances, or bodily or mental deterioration might force retirement from the activity, but in these instances, the passion is presumed still to be there. Being forced into a family caregiver role is one such extraneous circumstance. As an illustration of bodily deterioration, consider a friend of mine who had spent many years playing professional cello in a trio, but was driven by arthritis in his hands (a career contingency) to retire. It was the last thing he wanted to do.

But this is not the question I am raising here. Nor is burnout part of that question, since it cannot by definition occur in true devotee work; that is, it occurs only when devotees lose control over use and disposition of their time. Rather, it does happen—though I do not know how often—that the bloom simply falls off the rose; the worker or the leisure participant runs the course of the activity, getting out of it all that he believes is available for him. Now it is less fulfilling, perhaps on occasion even boring. Now it is time to search for a new activity, something the person at leisure can do, but the employed individual usually finds much more problematic. For the latter, the penalties of continuance commitment could well come into play at this time, not to mention the difficulty of finding another occupational passion and the months or years needed to work one's way into it to the point of experiencing deep fulfillment.

This is a very complicated area of human motivation in work and leisure, and we have very little research to go by. Indeed, some people seem to know no limits, as does economist Peter Drucker, now in his nineties, and conductor Kurt Masur, who at age seventy-five quit the New York Philharmonic to become music director of l'Orchestre National de France (*Calgary Herald*, 2002, p. B9). But, for others, fulfilling work or leisure opportunities may have dried up, caused by circumstances well beyond their control. Thus, organizational devotees sometimes get reassigned to new, but less interesting posts. Or some of the core tasks composing the posts they presently occupy get changed, say, by market trends or organizational restructuring. Yet, these people are typically in no position to search for other opportunities, be they in the local community or outside it. Marilyn Brooks, prominent Toronto clothing designer, closed her shop after forty years in a creative, devotee business that she loved. She had been a main force in creating Canada's fashion industry (Montanera, 2003, p. D12). One gets the impression from reading about her devotee career that it had simply lost its luster, particularly when contrasted with the serious leisure career she now plans to pursue. At age seventy she will return to painting, something in which she had hoped to find employment before she got into clothing design.

Alternatively, the devotee wants greater challenges than are presently available. This person's skill, knowledge, and experience have advanced well beyond what is needed; flow and other rewards have become too infrequent. This happens, for example, to talented professional athletes stuck in the minor leagues and to lawyers and physicians who mastered long ago the ways of handling the problems that their clients and patients routinely present.

Conclusions

The goal of this chapter, proceeding from the foundation laid down in the preceding one, has been to demonstrate how very much alike serious leisure and devotee work actually are. It further demonstrates how fundamentally dependent devotee work is on the domain of serious leisure. Bluntly put, without this leisure, the devotee occupations would never exist. This observation, when it comes to the trades and the client-centered professions, is obvious to most everyone, since they know of the preapprentice hobbyist and the preprofessional amateur. But when it comes to small businesses and the public-centered professions, it is, alas, sometimes overlooked. The student-amateur precursors of the former constitute a reasonably visible group, whereas the pure amateur-hobbyist-volunteer precursors of the latter are much less visible. With all the media hype surrounding professional athletes and entertainers, for instance, it is easy to forget that these people invariably come from a leisure background. Here they learned about their chosen field and their own taste and aptitude for it. Here is where their occupational devotion first took root.

At the amateur levels of pure and preprofessional and the hobbyist level of preapprentice, financial return, as already noted, is a minor, if not nonexistent, reward. The intrinsic, fulfilling aspects of the core activity combine to become the principal motivation in these areas. Still, any number of students preparing for work in professions known for their high levels of remuneration (e.g., law, medicine, engineering) think of a monetarily bright future. Moreover, some of them are headed into these occupations precisely for this reason. What, then, is the relationship between occupational devotion and getting paid to express it? When and where does the tendency emerge to sell one's devotee soul to the devil of high income?

6

Work, Leisure, and Money in Everyday Life

Money has been a problem for a long time. Sophocles, ancient Greek priest, general, and tragic poet, lamented in his drama *Antigone* that "there's nothing in the world so demoralizing as money." Accordingly, the first part of this chapter examines the bread and butter issue of getting paid to do devotee work. Are occupational devotees paid so they may work or is it the other way around? In the second part we look at the interweave of work and leisure in everyday life, both in general terms and in terms unique to the devotee.

Are They Paid so They May Work?

Most people, following the obverse thrust of this subtitle, work so they may be paid. When work is uninteresting, but still decently remunerative, workers can at least sustain life and, with whatever money that is leftover, enjoy a bit the smorgasbord of consumer opportunities that the commercial world lays out before them. A lifetime of uninteresting work is a high price to pay for economic survival and some spending cash, but many a modern worker enters into just this bargain with his educational qualifications and his personal standards for occupational success.

When work is highly attractive, however, this conventional orientation toward it and its remuneration often gets stood on its head. Still, the relationship of remuneration to devotee work is complicated, as is evident in the different economic situations that devotees live in or strive to live in.

Economic Situation

"Economic situation" is my term for the level of living made possible by a person's disposable wealth, that being in most instances

91

his occupational income but, in some instances, it includes returns on investments. Applied to occupational devotion, economic situation can be conceptualized as arrayed along a scale of increasing wealth that runs from poverty to opulence. The low end of the scale is anchored in *poverty* and *near poverty*, where the devotee is desperately trying to make a living, but so far with little monetary success. Here is the home of the starving artist and the minimally successful small business proprietor. Here money earned at devotee work is problematic only, though still very profoundly, in that there is little or none of it. Life is sustained by supplementary work, much of it more or less unskilled such as driving a taxi. Consider the old joke: "What do you say to the musicologist who knocks on your door one evening around dinner time?" The answer: "Thank's for the pizza, and here's a small tip."

With some financial success struggling artists and business people are wafted up the economic situation scale toward the level of *passable living*. Here they are joined by other kinds of occupational devotees, most of whom are just starting out in their chosen line of work and who have had the good fortune to avoid the poverty stage. Thus the *arriviste* artists and others share the passable living level with newly minted apprentice tradesmen, consultants and counselors fresh from university programs who have just hung out their shingles, and the owners of recently inaugurated small businesses who, from the beginning, have managed to turn a decent profit. Passable living consists, in the main, of having nutritious meals on a regular basis, lodging in a reasonably safe and healthy social and physical environment, and enough free time beyond work hours for adequate bodily maintenance (e.g., sleep, exercise) as well as relaxation and personal development through leisure.

With still greater monetary success, devotees enjoying a passable living may advance farther up the economic situation scale to the realm of *comfortable living*. Living comfortably builds on the base of passable living, by adding significant discretionary income with which to buy a variety of consumer goods that make life easier and more enjoyable than was possible during passable existence. This includes expanding one's personal definition of the good life to include acquisitions that go well beyond minimum standards, such as a house though an apartment would do, a Cadillac when a Ford would do, or designer clothes when mass produced apparel would do. Although many occupational devotees, in the course of their careers, eventually reach this level of economic existence, some actually start out more or less on it. Graduates from training programs in the most lucrative professions, among them law, medicine, engineering, and computer science, offer some fine examples. That is, unless they are saddled with huge school-related debts the retirement of which might force them into passable living for several years. And it is not impossible that, once in awhile, a devotee small business is a roaring success from the outset, as could happen with an instantly profitable restaurant or family farm (following a few good, back-to-back growing years).

At the top end of the economic situation scale lies *opulent living*. Devotees at these lofty heights enjoy amounts of discretionary cash far in excess of their counterparts at the next lowest level. Opulence permits conspicuous consumption. It also permits investments of various sorts, which in good economic times enable these devotees to acquire other sources of wealth in addition to the revenue they receive directly from pursuing the core activity of their occupation. This situation, we shall see shortly, also gives these devotees a certain flexibility, or margin of maneuver, when it comes to sticking to purely devotee activities or seeking extra income by working part of the time at less fulfilling, albeit decently, paying employment. Very few occupational devotees start out at this level, but some do advance this far up the economic situation scale. Most who do are in the sports and entertainment fields or, more rarely, one of the lucrative client-centered professions.

This economic situation scale is an objective tool, intended to help us understand how occupational devotees are distributed along the dimension of wealth. And, to give the scale greater precision, future empirical work in this area should include some quantitative measures of its levels of poverty, passable living, and so on. Meanwhile, subjectively speaking, individual devotees may define themselves differently, which is especially likely among those living passably or comfortably near the middle of the scale. For example, some devotees, just like some nondevotees, might be inclined to argue that, even if science objectively classifies them as enjoying a comfortable living, they are really only just getting by on the passable level.

Orientations toward Money

There are three critical orientations toward the question of pay for devotee work. One I will dub the *principled orientation*: occupational devotees and would-be devotees seek pay for pursuing their core activity, so they can do it more often than they can as serious leisure enthusiasts. They seek to be paid so they may work. The second orientation—define it as the *acquisitive orientation*—is that devotees and would-be devotees see their devotee occupation as offering a comfortable living, perhaps even an opulent one; that is, it is a job offering substantially greater remuneration than needed to live passably. They work so they may be paid; they see their remuneration as high enough to allow for an elevated standard living. The personal plan directing these devotees is to eventually abandon their fulfilling work for work returning substantial extrinsic rewards, thereby giving substance to Sophocles's observation. The third orientation combines the first two—call it the *principled-acquisitive orientation*; motivated by this disposition devotees seek to be paid so they may work, but at the same time, see no reason why they cannot sooner or later achieve at least a comfortable living into the bargain.

This is where occupational devotion is put to the test. At which point, if at any, does the devotee sell his occupational soul to the monetary devil? When does making more money take precedence over performing, more or less exclusively, fulfilling work?

Principled Devotee Work

Principled devotees search for little more than the minimum needed to routinely carry out their devotee work. That is, were more money than needed for this suddenly to become available, this type would not turn it down, unless accepting it impeded in some important way pursuit of the core activity. But money is not a supreme value for these devotees. What is of supreme value is being in a position to routinely carry out their fulfilling work and realize in their own way the five cultural values. In the social world of the principled devotees' occupation, they would be considered insiders. Moreover, they can only be fully principled while living passably, comfortably, or opulently. Devotees living in or near poverty are forced by their economic circumstances to seek money outside their core activity. They are principled part of the time but not all of the time, for they must perform a modicum of remunerated, nondevotee work so they may eat and pay the rent.

This way of establishing these top priorities of life is probably more easily effected in some fields than others. In the fine arts, where most devotees fall at or just above the low end of the economic situation scale, it is perhaps expedient to be principled in that there is, in any case, often little choice. This way of making a virtue of necessity is likely evident as well in some small businesses, particularly artistic craftwork, restoration and repair, and family farming on marginally productive soil. Still, casual observation suggests that principled devotees can be found in all four devotee areas. It is just that in occupations such as law and medicine, because of their normally higher remuneration, most devotees start out farther up the economic situation scale on or near the level of comfortable living.

The archetypical starving artist numbers among the principled devotees. Yet such people exist somewhere below the level of passable living. Typically, nutritious meals are not regularly available and lodging is substandard, in that it is neither reasonably safe nor properly located in a healthy social and physical environment. Some small business devotees find themselves in similar straits. In other words, starving artists and their equivalents in other occupations hope sooner or later to quit their Spartan life for one that can be qualified as at least passable, but not if that means abandoning substantially their devotee passion.

Acquisitive Devotee Work

Acquisitive devotees are, as devotees, here today but gone tomorrow, having used their fulfilling activity as a springboard to vault them into work capable of generating significant wealth. This hope for the pecuniary good life, acquired through devotee work, is most realistic in the professions and in some of the professional consulting and counseling fields. These devotees reason that here we have interesting, prestigious, yet fulfilling work at which we can eventually make plenty of money. The acquisitive orientation is strong in this instance, even if initial attraction to the devotee occupation, which is just as strong, is substantially framed as a desire for fulfillment. It is likely that, earlier in their careers, most acquisitive devotees pictured themselves as principled-acquisitive devotees, rather than purely acquisitive ones.

But, when lured by opportunities for generating ever more income, the typical acquisitive devotee, unlike his typical principled cousin, rarely says no. For some acquisitive devotees these opportunities involve further remunerated pursuit of the core activity. The dilemma here is that, in their thirst for more money, they drink in more work than they can handle, which as pointed out in the preceding chapter, tends to quickly water down its fulfilling qualities. The job has now spun out of the individual's control, losing its appeal in the process. The university professor who gets into the predicament of trying to write at the same time two contracted textbooks risks falling into this trap. Writing texts can certainly be fulfilling, but that effect quickly wears off in face of too many publishers' deadlines.

Additionally, in some professional fields, opportunities arise that can charm money-oriented, acquisitive devotees away from their fulfilling work. The fine arts professions are particularly susceptible to this siren call, where it is commonly referred to as "going commercial." Many a serious painter, novelist, jazzman, and symphony musician has been unable to resist the chance to make much more money producing something that sells well to a sizeable segment of the general public. Though some acquisitive devotees manage to keep a hand in their devotee art while profiting mightily in its commercial wing, those most stirred by the appeal of opulent living carry on into a full-time quest for financial success, with the initial devotee work eventually being abandoned. Jazz trumpeter Miles Davis went through his final years as a rock musician (albeit with some links to jazz), as did singer Rosemary Clooney, who, though also initially a jazz artist, wound up singing pop until late in her career when she returned to her original passion.

Organizationally based occupational devotees sometimes have to deal with their own alluring calls for greater income that, if heeded, threaten the pursuit of their core devotee activity. Though said in chapter 5 to be rare in today's mid- and large-sized bureaucracies, the few true devotee professionals employed here do sometimes get recruited to positions that remove them altogether from their devotee work. A substantially higher salary is one justification for making this career change, which may, however, come at great cost to intrinsic job satisfaction. Some devotees who make this jump may also be attracted by the prestige and the perquisites that go with posts higher in the organization's structure, such as those of dean, director, or vice president.

Acquisitive devotees may even turn up in the world of small business. This happens when the little enterprise becomes so successful that its owner begins to think of expanding it. There are doubtlessly many reasons for contemplating such growth, with the possibility of making considerably more money clearly being one of them. But expansion is accompanied by many new challenges that, together, will surely force the devotee entrepreneur to abandon his core activity. For instance, because this person must now oversee operations in more offices than previously, there will now be little or no time for the love of repairing glass and ceramic objects or working with dating files.

Construction workers who start their own enterprise in, say, plumbing, painting, or plastering, can eventually meet up with similar problems. To the extent that these new businesses succeed, they will need to hire more tradesmen to carry out the core activity. This, in turn, will engender more paperwork and managerial problems, which are bound sooner or later to take the owner from the field and the core activity to the office and the world of administration.

Principled-Acquisitive Devotee Work

Principled-acquisitive devotees not only hope to find great financial success doing fulfilling work, they also manage to achieve exactly that. Some, like the acquisitive devotees, probably start their amateur or hobbyist years inspired by this vision. Others, as they realize their own potential in their chosen field and see how it might pay off financially in the future, begin only then to, in effect, view themselves as principled-acquisitive devotees.

Highly economically successful professionals who still work as devotees have succeeded in retaining control over the flow of their fulfilling work. They have managed to become well paid for doing something that has the appeal of leisure, a rare situation indeed in modern society. Occupational devotees are uncommon enough, but those who do well financially are in even shorter supply. It is as if employers, in particular, and society, in general, know intuitively that people whose work is a passion will, other things equal, settle for substantially lower remuneration than those whose work is in some major way disagreeable. In harmony with this assumption we

have seen that many occupational devotees, like their serious leisure counterparts, regard the reward of monetary return as of secondary importance, compared with such rewards as self-enhance-
ment, self-actualization, and group accomplishment. And perhaps
these devotees (both principled and principled-acquisitive) know
intuitively that life is good with their present work, and that it could
be a lot worse were they to take up a nondevotee occupation, even if
it pays a much better salary.

This raises the question of whether occupational devotees are being
exploited by their employers. Surely, some must feel this way, when
they see what others are being paid who have similar qualifications
and levels of experience. And in some occupations this gap may be
partially reduced through collective pressure from a trade union or
similar wage bargaining unit. The effect of this action, to the extent
it succeeds, is to push principled devotees toward, and perhaps even
into, the class of principled-acquisitive devotees. But in the university world, where the charge of exploitation is possibly most often
voiced and is perhaps most valid, such collective pressure, though
usually possible, is by no means always effective. Of the huge range
of occupations represented in a typical North American university,
the vast majority have a variety of opposite numbers in government
and industry, where pay levels are generally significantly higher
than in the universities. So, here, the exploitation thesis has some
validity. But there is also a subtle counterargument: occupational
devotees, including those in universities, already receive significant rewards for their work (i.e., those discussed in chaps. 4 and 5),
rewards that many nondevotee workers wish they had. This ineq-
uity, it could be argued, is offset, at least to some extent, by giving a
higher wage to the latter than to the former.

The criterion of control over the amount and disposition of time
put into fulfilling work enforces a sort of upper limit on the category of principled-acquisitive devotee. There are no doubt famous
and hence frequently sought out, surgeons, architects, criminal lawyers, and the like who retain such control and thereby remain solid
members of this category. They are in a position to refuse all but the
most appealing work and to hold that work to a manageable level.
But what about the renowned athletes and entertainers who work
for organizations that have substantial say in when and where they
work?

It might appear, at first blush, that the multimillion-dollar players in football, baseball, hockey, and basketball, exemplify well, if not ideally, the principled-acquisitive occupational devotee. Yet in fact, they have lost significant control over disposition of the time they spend at their trade. For with such high wages their owners are strongly inclined to force them to play as much as possible, and to arrange for seasons filled with a sufficient number of matches to bring amounts of money required to offset those wages. The result is that all players, the most highly paid included, play in a given season far more of their sport than they would like. This is not, however, a question of career boredom of the sort discussed in chapter 5. Rather, if my study of amateur and professional football players in Canada is any indication (Stebbins, 1993, p. 96), it is the boredom (and fatigue) that accumulates with the extended participation in practice sessions that roll on inexorably between each match. By contrast, the matches themselves were said to be exciting whenever they were scheduled during the season.

In fact, the players in heavily commercialized sports often lose effective control over the conditions of their own sport participation. These conditions come under the control of general managers, team owners, corporate sponsors, advertisers, media personnel, marketing and publicity staff, professional management staff, accountants, and agents. The organizations that control commercial sports are intended to coordinate the interests of all these people, but their primary goal is to maximize revenues. This means that organizational decisions generally reflect the combined economic interests of many people having no direct personal connection with a sport or the athletes involved in it. The power to affect these decisions is grounded in resources that many not be connected with sports. Therefore, athletes in many commercial sports find themselves cut out of decision-making processes, even when the decisions affect their health and the rewards they receive for playing (Coakley, 2001, p. 328).

But how about players of individual sports, who would seem to be more in control of their own work? They are, after all, not owned by a team. The top ones do have important sponsorships, however, arrangements that place significant control of their professional lives in the hands of other people. Being financially tied thus to an equipment manufacturer, for instance, creates dependence on that company. Furthermore, to realize its investments in its sponsored players, the company often tells the latter when, where, and how often they will play.

In short, a good case can be made for the rich and famous in the world of sport that they are not occupational devotees at all. Instead, the purest devotees in the professional athlete class are to be found among the unsung, unsponsored journeymen of individual sport. Their economic situation, depending on their ranking in their sport, ranges from passable to comfortable living. Meanwhile, in popular team sports, even the journeymen lack significant control over their work, since they, too, must play through seasons the length of which is certainly not of their making.

It is much the same with top entertainers, at least for those tied to an agent (and most are). Additionally, they may have, much like highly visible, professional athletes, a personal manager, an accountant, and the recurrent need to deal with media people and marketing and publicity personnel. Thus they, too, lose their grip on their devotee attachment to their occupation, suggesting, as just done with athletes, that here, as well, the true devotee is to be found primarily among the lesser and more ordinarily remunerated souls.

Work and Leisure in Everyday Life

In this section we explore the work and leisure lifestyles of occupational devotees and the interweaving of these two. It was observed in chapter 4, where the concept of lifestyle was presented in detail, that it consists of a distinctive set of shared patterns of tangible behavior that springs up around a set of coherent interests or social conditions or both. Moreover, lifestyles are explained and justified by a set of related values (in this instance the five cultural values), attitudes, and orientations.

Uncontrollability and Selfishness

One of the many properties that serious leisure shares with devotee work is the tendency toward uncontrollability. For instance, I learned that the amateurs in my studies of astronomy and football, having spent the evening before observing stars or playing a game, often found themselves in a less than optimal condition for work the next day. I also learned that it is always tempting to increase the time available for amateur interests by subtracting a few hours from work or nonwork obligations, if not from other leisure activities. Indeed, a professional violinist used to counsel his daughter, "Rachel, never marry an amateur violinist! He will want to play quartets all night" (from Bowen, 1935, p. 93). For those who find the small and occasional monetary rewards of amateurism attractive, this tendency is only exacerbated. Then there is the universal desire to upgrade: to own a better set of golf clubs, to buy a more powerful telescope, to take more dance lessons perhaps from a renowned (and consequently more expensive) professional, and so forth. The same applies to hobbyist and volunteer pursuits. Indeed, serious leisure activity in general stands ready to devour all the practitioners' time and money.

The tendency toward uncontrollability is likely found in various forms of casual leisure as well, should we look carefully. But the complement of that observation is the one that uncontrollability is nonetheless significantly greater among serious leisure participants in all fields, particularly the most enthusiastic of them, than among, for example, dabblers or spectators. The widespread, highly attractive opportunity for personal fulfillment in serious leisure is, in part, what makes it especially uncontrollable. And that it is so prominent a lifestyle issue in serious leisure suggests that the same is also true in devotee work.

Some devotees may have help from their employers in buying top-flight equipment, in attending conferences, in purchasing books, and so on, while others enjoy no such support. Thus, both the symphony violinist and the amateur quartet player would love to have better instruments, and both will have to realize this dream using their own resources. In fact, amateurs receiving high salaries from their "day job" are likely in a better financial position to buy a fine old violin than the run-of-the-mill professional.

The problem of uncontrollability also finds expression in the expenditure of time. Chances are good that a particular devotee, like his serious leisure counterpart, will be eager to spend more time at the core activity than will be countenanced by certain significant others who also makes demands on that time. They soon come to understand that the devotee is, from time to time, working beyond what his employer requires and, for all that, perhaps not even making any more money. Charges of selfishness may not be long in coming.

I found in my research on serious leisure that attractive activity and selfishness are natural partners (Stebbins, 2001a, chap. 4). But selfishness enacted with reference to serious leisure interests, and now we add devotee work, is qualitatively different in at least four ways from selfish casual leisure.

One, when contrasted with the casual form, serious leisure is nearly always much more complicated and, for this reason, often takes up much more of the participant's time. Routine participation in a serious leisure or devotee career in theatre, ceramics, writing novels, or playing tennis is a much more detailed and socially complex undertaking than the routine practice of sun tanning, hot tubbing, strolling in the park, or imbibing at weekend beer parties. The first commonly encourages expenditures of time so extensive that the close friends and relatives of the self-seeker sometimes see them as cutting into the time they hold to be rightfully theirs. These special others may lose some of their cherished work or leisure rewards, because certain significant people in their lives regularly and frequently devote themselves to a type of serious leisure or devotee work.

Two, some types of serious leisure and devotee work can only be pursued within a rigid schedule which, it turns out, allow little room for compromise vis-à-vis types that can be pursued at personally convenient times. Imputations of selfishness are considerably more likely to arise with regard to the first. Here, for instance, devotees and participants alike must attend regularly scheduled dance rehearsals or basketball practices. People who can turn to their painting, stamp collecting, craft production, or reading of Shakespeare's works when no pressure exists to do something else are certainly less open to being denounced by, for example, spouse or partner for behaving selfishly.

Continuing in the same vein, differences in amount and kind of selfishness even show up across the three types of serious leisure. Volunteering, with its roots in altruism, appears to be relatively free of selfish exploitation of the public being served. And it is possible that the altruistic attitude weakens or even eliminates the tendency to treat others selfishly while arranging to volunteer. But where this internal control is weaker, as in the more purely self-interested pursuit of a hobby or an amateur activity, there appears to be, compared with volunteering, more exploitation of such people as family, friends, and neighbours, as they define this situation.

Three, we can make a similar observation with reference to devotee work and serious and casual leisure activities that exclude one's partner vis-à-vis those that include that person. Logically, it is difficult to complain about alter's selfishness if ego also participates in the same work or leisure and finds it more or less equally fulfilling. I found considerable variation in serious leisure in this regard, with fields such as music and archaeology being more amenable to family participation than those such as theatre and barbershop singing (Stebbins, 1992, pp. 109-111). On the casual leisure side we can classify as inclusive family activities swimming, ice skating, picnicking, and dining out and as exclusive individual activities same-sex gatherings, meetings of select-membership organizations, and attendance at events aimed at either a male or a female clientele. Depending on how often and how regularly people pursue exclusive work and leisure activities, these activities are more likely than inclusive activities to spawn allegations of selfishness.

Four, devotee work and serious leisure, compared with casual leisure, are often more debatable as selfishness, when seen from the standpoints of both victim of the selfishness and self-seeker. Devotees and serious leisure enthusiasts alike have at their fingertips as justifications for their actions such venerated ideals as self-enrichment, self-expression, and self-actualization as well as service to others, contribution to group effort, development of a valued personal identity, and regeneration of oneself after work. Continuous effort to realize the five cultural values is also a respected personal mission. These ideals can be used to justify such practices as routine solitude, long hours away from home, big expenditures of money, and occasional use of others' precious resources, all of which can be carried out in ways simultaneously regarded as exploitative by victims.

Leisure Lifestyle of Devotees

With remarks like those just made about the uncontrollability of serious leisure and devotee work, you might wonder if observations on the leisure lifestyle of the latter are, at bottom, little more than academic. But occupational devotees do know leisure, even if only of the casual variety. Some of this leisure is probably forced on them by close friends and relatives, possibly amid charges of selfishness (making such activity more an obligation than genuine leisure), but some of it is also likely intentionally sought. In the latter situation devotees have for the moment exhausted themselves at their occupational passion.

Although casual leisure cannot compare in depth of fulfillment with devotee work, it does have its important benefits (Stebbins, 2001c).

- One lasting benefit of casual leisure is the creativity and discovery it sometimes engenders. Serendipity, the quintessential form of informal experimentation, accidental discovery, and spontaneous invention, usually underlies these two processes. Such creativity and discovery does not result from trying to solve a problem, which instead, is often approached using exploration (Stebbins, 2001b).

- "Edutainment" is another benefit. It springs from participation in mass entertainment, including watching films and television, listening to popular music, reading mass books and articles, and attending theme parks. Inadvertently, while doing these things, participants learn something of substance about the social and physical world in which they live. They are, in a word, entertained and educated in the same breath (Nahrstedt, 2000).

- Casual Leisure also affords regeneration, or re-creation, possibly even more so than its counterpart, serious leisure, since the latter is often intense. Such relaxation and entertainment can have enduring effects, since they help enhance general equanimity, particularly between periods of concentrated activity.

- Another benefit that can arise from casual leisure is the development and maintenance of interpersonal relationships. One of its types, sociable conversation, is particularly fertile in this regard, but other types, when shared, including sensory stimulation and passive and active entertainment, can also have this effect.

- Well-being is still another benefit that can flow from experiencing casual leisure. This occurs when a person achieves an optimal leisure lifestyle, defined as the deeply satisfying pursuit during free time of one or more substantial, absorbing forms of serious leisure, complemented by a judicious amount of casual leisure. A person finds an optimal leisure lifestyle by engaging in leisure activities that separately and in combination realize human potential and enhance quality of life and well being (Stebbins, 2000b).

Serious leisure is different, however. Its allure is as hard to resist for an occupational devotee as for a nondevotee. Indeed, as I have observed elsewhere (Stebbins, 2000a), the spirit of professional work is such that those who have it expect more from their leisure than the casual variety can provide. That is, only serious leisure can return the kinds of rewards they find in their devotee work. Whatever the amount of free time at their disposal, the research I have reviewed in this area suggests that, to the degree it is felt, the spirit of professional work profoundly influences activities there. Professionals with this orientation are, when not at work, stimulated to look for more or less equally fulfilling activities, to search in this sphere for still other central life interests where they can experience the equivalent of the spirit of professional work. As a result, their activities during leisure, retirement and, for some, unemployment are likewise distinguished by their exceptionally fulfilling qualities.

Thus inspired—to convert virtually all of nonobligated life into the pursuit of deep fulfillment—occupational devotees do show up in a wide range of serious leisure pursuits. In the past and the present, physicians, for example, have formed their own community orchestras and jazz ensembles. In my studies over the years of amateurs, hobbyists, and career volunteers, I have met a variety of professionals, tradesmen, and small business proprietors, many of whom seemed to have as much passion for their livelihood as for the serious leisure on which they were being interviewed. True, many occupational devotees, once finished for the day with their work, simply prefer to collapse in hedonic pleasure provided by some sort of casual leisure (likely these days to be watching television or a video or browsing the web). The thought of doing anything as engaging as their work is flatly out of the question.

This brings us to the matter of the proportion of people, in general, and occupational devotees, in particular, who go in for serious leisure. My answer to this question, which is raised often, has been that, on average, 20 percent of the adult population in North America participates in some sort of serious leisure. This figure may be higher or lower for particular activities, in that golf, for instance, might attract 30 percent while darts accounts for only 10 percent. Remember that, here, we are speaking of true serious leisure participants, not dabblers and dilettantes in or casual spectators of serious leisure activities.

This is, however, a crude estimate, based on my impressions gained from observing North American society over the thirty years that I have devoted to studying this phenomenon. Unfortunately, such impressions are all we have to go on. As far as I know, no agency, public or private, has ever conducted a survey of serious leisure participation per se. True, serious leisure activities are included in many a general survey of leisure participation, but being unaware of the idea of serious leisure, these surveys conflate it and casual participation in the same activity. Thus is it of little help to the student of serious leisure to learn that, in a given year, 35 percent of the adult population plays tennis ten times or more. Ten times is hardly enough for serious participation, and what, in any case, is the nature of the participation? Are these players simply batting the ball back and forth over the net, or are they actually playing a match but with no real seriousness? Or are they members of a tennis club playing each other to experience some of the ten rewards mentioned earlier and realize some of the five cultural values?

Further, is this 20 percent estimate any different for occupational devotees and their participation in serious leisure? The argument just made about its appeal for these busy people throws partial support on both sides of this estimate. Thus many professionals appear to have developed high expectations for their leisure, having found high fulfillment in their work; for them anything less seems anticlimactic. Florida (2002, p. 169) writes more generally that, among creative people, the old conformist lifestyle "has given way to a more creative one based on the eyes-wide-open pursuit of wide-ranging, highly engaging [leisure] activities and stimuli." Yet, following a very full day of devotee work, does time and energy realistically exist for serious leisure? All considered, my hunch is that twenty percent may be too high for occupational devotees, but a proper survey—one founded on good definitions of serious and casual leisure—would certainly shed some light on the question.

Occupational devotees have some good reasons for not pursuing serious leisure, in that they have comparatively little free time, and have already realized in their work many powerful cultural values and social and personal rewards. But what about the working nondevotees, especially those blessed with ample free time? They appear to be doing little to raise the 20 percent figure, a tendency explained, in part, by the fact that they are often unaware of the serious leisure available to them. In this state of ignorance they are unable to become involved in it, no matter how accessible it is or what their taste and aptitude for it and no matter that they might have sufficient money to pursue a number of its activities.

There is, furthermore, the ever-present question of motivation. By no means everyone is inclined to "work" hard at any activity. Two of the six defining characteristics of serious leisure are perseverance and putting in enough effort to gain needed skill, knowledge, and experience. Such requirements tend to separate sheep from goats; they also help maintain the 20 percent figure. Many a respondent in my studies of serious leisure remarked that, when discussing with friends their leisure passion, those friends often responded that such intense involvement "sounds like work." In other words, for their free time, it is clearly not their cup of tea. Indeed, for occupational devotees these leisure activities *are* work, a livelihood that is.

Conclusions

It is interesting that most people tend to reject highly fulfilling involvement in serious leisure, while nevertheless widely proclaiming their interest in finding its equivalent in an occupation. Many reasons exist for this curious hypocrisy. They include the view held by many Americans and Canadians that leisure is essentially and exclusively a hedonic good time—it is casual leisure—and that persevering and putting in effort there is simply not their idea of what to do when free of obligations. Another reason is that some work, especially the best work, requires just such an orientation, so why not make the most of it and try to find a job that is fulfilling. Of course, it is also true, and this is a third reason, that having learned about one or more devotee occupations, some people are unwilling to persevere and do what they must to acquire the necessary skill, knowledge, and experience to find fulfillment there or even to obtain the basic educational credentials needed to get started. This group is populated with the dropouts from college and university instructional programs, and for those who do manage to complete such programs, the occupational "deadwood" who come to their devotee occupation with the attitude of a nondevotee.

Thus true occupational devotees are not likely to renounce their work for an early retirement or a part-time working arrangement, simply to pursue more or less full-time a serious leisure passion. They may have such a passion, as already indicated, but in any conflict between powerful work and leisure passions, the former seems destined to win out, at least until enthusiasm for it has run its course (see the Marilyn Brooks example in chap. 5) or external circumstances conspire to seriously efface the devotee's quality of work life.

In the final analysis, it is evident that we have in the occupational devotee a valuable community resource. People who are highly trained and experienced in a core activity holding significant utility for the collectivity and are at peace with themselves and the world around them because of the fulfilling nature of their work contribute mightily to the society in which they live and operate. Though present signs are not very encouraging that we will be able to produce conditions attractive to new devotees and the retention of existing ones, we should, in this regard, be doing all we can. They are an enormously valuable resource. To the extent that we fail at this task, and it looks as if we will in some significant degree, serious leisure will have to fill the gaps for would-be devotees cast aside by whatever decline there will be in the number of devotee occupations. In short, the interplay of serious leisure and devotee work will become even more important in the future than it is now.

7

Common Ground in Separate Worlds: Some Implications

Seeing devotee work and serious leisure as compatible occupants of a common terrain rather than as estranged inhabitants living in two separate worlds has numerous implications for society and the individual. In general, the fact that devotee work and serious leisure are really two sides of the same coin (see below in this chapter) enables us to consider several questions in broader, more profound terms than heretofore. Now the two can be viewed from both a work and a leisure angle, when before this these questions were addressed from only one of these perspectives, with precious little reference to the other. Four areas can benefit from assessed from the common ground of devotee work and serious leisure: well-being, bureaucracy and alienation, the Information Age, and serious leisure as a substitute for work.

Well-Being

Personal well-being is a major by-product of much of serious leisure. And following the line of reasoning used throughout this book, the same must therefore be true of devotee work. But the first question to pose in this section is whether even a serious leisure activity, which is not coerced, can engender well-being when it is also engenders certain costs and occupies a marginal status *vis-à-vis* the three social institutions of work, leisure, and family. The answer is, yes, it can. For, to the extent that well-being is fostered by fulfillment through everyday life activities, research evidence suggests that it is an important by-product of serious leisure (Haworth, 1986; Haworth and Hill, 1992; Mannell, 1994). As additional evidence the respondents in my several studies of serious leisure, when interviewed, invariably described in detail and with great enthusiasm the profound satisfaction they derive from their amateur, hobbyist, and volunteer activities. There is every reason to believe that occupational devotees find the same feelings of well-being through involvement in their core activities.

All this evidence is, however, only correlational. No one has yet carried out a properly controlled study expressly designed to ascertain whether long-term involvement in a form of serious leisure or devotee work actually leads to significant and enduring increases in feelings of well-being. The extent to which serious leisure can generate major interpersonal role conflict for some practitioners—it led to two divorces among the twenty-five respondents in a study of amateur theater (Stebbins, 1979, pp. 81-83; on family conflict in running, see also Goff, Flick, and Oppliger, 1997)—should be sufficient warning to avoid postulating an automatic link between these two kinds of leisure and work, on the one hand, and well-being, on the other. I also have anecdotal evidence that serious leisure activities can generate intrapersonal conflict, such as when people fail to establish priorities among their many and varied leisure interests or among those interests and their devotee work. This implies that even an approach-approach conflict between cherished leisure and work activities may possibly affect unfavorably well-being. Hamilton-Smith (1995, pp. 6-7) says our lack of knowledge about the link between serious leisure and well-being is a major lacuna in contemporary leisure research. The same lack is evident in the study of occupational devotion.

Finally, are we being realistic when we argue that serious leisure or devotee work is a primary source of personal well-being in life? There is probably no sphere in life where well-being can take root and grow in pure and undiluted form. In other words, I suspect that when we are aglow with feelings of well-being, whether at work, during leisure or while performing extrawork obligations, we are, in effect, experiencing those feelings as significant profit of rewards against costs.

Moreover, what is noteworthy about the theoretical link between any kind of leisure and well-being is that, in common sense, we seldom expect costs in the former, whereas we routinely expect them at work (even devotee work) and during the execution of obligatory tasks. That we expect to find pure enjoyment everywhere in our leisure, however unrealistic this expectation, may be shown some day to have a powerful effect on how much we feel fulfilled with the serious leisure we are pursuing. And when a sense of well-being does emerge here—as it surely will—this expectation will influence the level of intensity with which that well-being is felt. Certainly, we can describe a serious pursuit or activity as either mildly or highly fulfilling.

Although serious leisure and devotee work when married to well-being would seem to make two perfect couples, it is likely that these two relationships will be found to be far more complex than current levels of theory and research suggest.

Alienation and Bureaucracy

Whether experienced at work or at leisure, well-being in the modern world is a precarious feeling, subject as it is to the pernicious effects of bureaucratization and alienating tasks. Little has been said so far in this book about alienation, chiefly because it cannot coexist with either occupational devotion or serious leisure. When workers are alienated, devotion to their work is impossible. "Bad work," says Schumacher (1980, p. 27), alienates workers both from themselves and their work. Alienating work springs from enacting a core activity that is merely extrinsically rewarding, in that, for example, it allows little or no originality or discretion and generates scant fulfillment. Furthermore, alienation is no longer exclusively associated with blue-collar work, as it once was; it may now be growing not only there but also in some professional occupations once known for the fulfillment they offered. Over-bureaucratization of, for example, volunteer work can also generate alienation, not infrequently manifested as burnout. But note an important work/leisure difference here: compared with devotees the noncoerced volunteers can more easily quit their alienating role, and many do just that.

Aronowitz and DiFazio (1994, pp. 197-198) hold that two increasingly powerful constraints are transforming the devotee work of some organizational professionals into work that is increasingly alienating.

> Insofar as they are employed by bureaucratic organizations— public agencies, large law firms and corporations—the range of decision making to which they have access is narrowed; and technological change has recomposed their jobs so that, for most employees, their training exceeds the requirements of job performance. For example, a

physician affiliated with a large research hospital in New York City reported to one of
the authors that patient care is increasingly governed by computerized information.
(Aronowitz and DiFazio, 1994, p. 97)

The computer, especially when used to serve the goals and strate-
gies of large, bureaucratized organizations, is capable of substantially trivializing many challenging, fulfilling core activities. Badly
conceived technology is also occasionally a problem, in that the
core task is attractive, while electronic implementation of certain
aspects of it are clumsy or inefficient. In deciding to deskill particular functions and implement computerized operations, cash-strapped
companies and government agencies believe they are saving money,
such as that paid out for salaries, and in the same effort, enhancing
efficiency. Moreover, the appeal of this strategy at the managerial
level appears to be spreading.

The Information Age

This raises the question of how much genuine devotee work is
likely to be available in the Information Age, which has already un-
leashed forces inimical to much of it. It also raises the question of
the role of serious leisure in this epoch and how the common ground
shared by these two can help better the human condition.

In the industrialized world of today, there is more time after work
than ever. Still, it was true for awhile in the United States, as Schor
(1991) concluded in *The Overworked American*, that many workers
were so eager to make money to buy coveted consumer items that,
whenever possible, they took second jobs or worked overtime. And
when not making money they could try to save it, most notably by
taking on do-it-yourself projects. But after meeting the multitude of
obligations they had set for themselves, these drudges soon discovered that they had scarcely any free time. Only four years later,
however, Howe (1995) claimed that this attitude was changing;
now more and more American workers were emphasizing "reasoned wellness," while backing off from their earlier greed and
narcissism. She held that they were also beginning to endow family time with the same level of importance as work and other
forms of obligated time. In a similar vein, Samuel (1994, p. 48)
described the tendency observed by Schor as a "temporary development" in the United States that stood out against the worldwide
trend toward increased free time.

Overall, American research does support the claim that the after-work time of many people has been growing in both amount and significance (Robinson and Godbey, 1997). But, oddly, this research also suggests that some of them feel more rushed than ever. Zuzanek (1996, p. 65) provides the clearest statement yet of this paradox. "In general, US time-budget findings parallel those of Canada, and provide additional evidence of the complexity of life in modern industrial societies marked, as it seems, by concurrent trends toward greater time freedom as well as 'harriedness' and 'time pressure.'" And this general trend continues despite the present tendency in a number of industries for managers to wring many extra hours of service from their full-time salaried and hourly-rated employees alike. Yet, the size of this group of reluctantly overworked employees is shrinking, as more and more of their positions are lost in the nearly universal quest by managers to organize as much as possible along electronic lines the work for which they are responsible.

Lefkowitz (1979) prefigured this trend—the substantial reduction of life's work and nonwork obligations. His interviews, conducted during the late 1970s, suggested that a small but growing number of Americans were expanding their leisure involvements by voluntarily accepting unemployment, partial employment, or early retirement. Two years later Yankelovich (1981) confirmed these impressions in a nationwide survey of Americans. Today, the evidence, which was presented earlier, clearly supports the proposition that the work ethic of old has waned in intensity, even in North America, by far the home of the largest number of its adherents.

But today, paralleling the tendency to voluntarily reduce obligations, is a much stronger force: the technologically driven, involuntary reduction of paid work. In *The End of Work* Jeremy Rifkin (1995) describes the current decline in the size of the global labor pool and the traditional market economy, and how both forces are now pushing ever larger numbers of people toward greater free time at an alarming rate, whatever the individual's interest in reducing his or her level of work. As the twenty-first century dawns, a wide variety of employable men and women are finding that their job opportunities have shrunk, sometimes to nothing at all. Behind these unsettling trends lie the powerful forces of what Rifkin calls the "Third Industrial Revolution": the far-reaching effects of electronic technology as manifested in the microcircuitry of computers, robotics, telecommunications, and similar devices.

The Information Age has dawned. In it, Rifkin observes, these technologies will continue well into the twenty-first century inexorably replacing workers, either directly or indirectly, in virtually every sector of the economy, including manufacturing, transportation, agriculture, government, and the retail and financial services. New jobs will be created in significant number only in the knowledge sector, in science, computing, consulting, education, and the technical and professional services directly related to the new technology. Rifkin says this sector will compose no more than twenty percent of the workforce. Jobs lost in other sectors will be gone forever, offset very little by the comparatively small number of jobs generated in the knowledge sector. Furthermore, occupational retraining is no solution, for the people in line for such retraining generally lack the necessary educational background on which to build the skills and information they would need to work in the knowledge sector. In short, regardless of the orientation of modern men and women toward life after work, they now seem destined to have much more of that life than ever. Other authors writing in the same vein, such as Aronowitz and DiFazio (1994) and Howard (1995), stand as proof that Rifkin is not alone in observing these trends.

And, speaking of life after work, these writers have failed to address themselves to this matter, apart from putting forward two broad observations, one tantalizing, the other frightening. They predict that the Information Age will offer greatly expanded opportunities for leisure and personal development by way of it and that this Age will offer free time far in excess of the typical person's capacity to use it constructively. Seen from the standpoint of the person trying to adapt to a world buffeted by momentous change, these observers paint a picture of life after work in the Information Age that is both too hazy and too unsettling for comfort.

Devotee Work

The devotee occupations, a significant proportion of which are found in the knowledge industries, will surely continue to be an important part of the economy of industrialized countries. I pointed out in chapter 2 that the scope of devotee work has nonetheless shrunk in some ways. It has been buffeted by such forces as occupational deskilling, degradation, and industrial restructuring (e.g., downsizing). Deindustrialization (e.g., plant closure and relocation), failed job improvement programs, and overwork, whether required by employers or sought by workers craving extra income, have also taken their toll. Still, certain forms of devotion are more evident today than heretofore, seen for instance, in the rise of the independent consultant and counselor and the part-time professional. Nor is there any reason to suspect that small businesses or trades workers will decline in proportion or absolute number. Yet, there are constraints on professionals of the kind considered earlier.

So the problem appears to be less one of continued devotee work opportunities than one of a narrowing recruitment base for people to fill those opportunities. It was just noted that new jobs will be created in significant number, but only in the knowledge sector. Jobs lost in the other sectors will be gone forever, offset very little by the comparatively small number of jobs generated in the knowledge sector. And occupational retraining was said to be no solution, since people in line for such retraining generally lack the necessary educational background on which to build the skills and information they would need to work in the knowledge sector.

These labor market trends are not apparent in the small business and skilled trades spheres of occupational devotion. Newcomers will enter this kind of devotee work much as they have in the past, and no decrease in the proportions doing so seems likely. But substantial numbers of those who would like to break into the professional (consulting, counseling) part of the knowledge sector will find this difficult to do. Frustrated thus in their quest for fulfilling work, what will they do next? Having set their hearts on the cherished values of achievement, success, freedom, activity and work, and individual personality, where will these people go to realize them? In other words, what does the future hold for people who are keen to realize these values? Does this signal a return to the roots of occupational devotion, to serious leisure?

Serious Leisure as a Substitute for Work

If serious leisure can be the precursor of the devotee occupations, it can also be the refuge for those no longer able to participate in them or those who were, by circumstances, denied the opportunity to enter them in the first place. True, occupational devotees qua leisure participants will not get paid so they may work, but they will find all the fulfilling qualities they were seeking in a devotee occupation. Here there is common ground, which revolves around deeply appealing core activities.

Let us start by returning to the concept of social world introduced in chapter 1, the set of characteristic groups, events, routines, practices, and organizations, which is held together, to an important degree, by semiformal, or mediated, communication. The social world is not only a concept well in tune with the work and leisure routines of the present and future, it is also a desideratum of many a modern man and woman both for today and for the years to come. If people can no longer find a work organization to belong to or can only belong marginally to one as an outside consultant or part-time employee how, then, can they become part of the community, whether conceived of locally, regionally, nationally, or internationally? Increasingly, it appears that the only available communal connections for most people will come through activities taking place in their after-work time. Yet, because they tend to be private, purely family activities rarely generate such connections. But those who once found meaningful organizational ties at work can still turn to serious leisure, where one of the principal attractions of most of the amateur, hobbyist, and volunteer activities is the sense of being part of a bustling, fascinating, all-encompassing social world. For many enthusiasts their involvement in this entity is as exciting as the central activity itself and, in career volunteer work, often indistinguishable from it.

The routine of some serious leisure can constitute yet another appealing feature for those with severely shortened workweeks or no work at all. A wide variety of amateur and hobbyist activities require regular practice, rehearsal, or participation sessions, and volunteers are often asked to serve at their posts during certain hours on certain days of the week. People who miss the routine of the full-time job will find an attractive equivalent in any number of serious leisure pursuits.

Substitute Lifestyle and Identity

We also saw earlier that serious leisure offers both a major lifestyle and a respected identity for its participants, and I should now like to add that both can serve as solid substitutes for the ones they once knew in their work. Moreover, some lifestyles serve to identify their participants. In other words, the participants are members of a category of humankind who recognize themselves and, to some extent, are recognized by the larger community for the distinctive mode of life they lead. This is certainly true for regulars in some of the casual leisure pursuits (e.g., beach dwellers, casino gamblers) as well as enthusiasts in many of the serious leisure activities (e.g., inveterate alpine skiers and amateur actors).

It was observed in chapter 1 that a profound lifestyle awaits anyone routinely pursuing a serious leisure career in, say, amateur science, volunteer work with the mentally handicapped, the hobby of model railroading, or that of mountain climbing. And this person may also find exciting, albeit obviously less profound, lifestyles in such casual leisure pastimes as socializing in the local pub and drinking with golfing associates at the "nineteenth hole." But many other forms of casual leisure, for example, beachcombing or window-shopping, are seldom shared with large numbers of other people; therefore they fail to qualify as group lifestyles as set out previously. Moreover, in themselves and where lifestyle is part of identity, these activities are too superficial and unremarkable to serve as the basis for a recognizable mode of living.

Substitute Central Life Interest

To the extent that lifestyles form around complicated, absorbing, satisfying activities, as they invariably do in serious leisure, they can also be viewed as behavioral expressions of the participants' central life interests in those activities. Robert Dubin (1992) defines this interest as "that portion of a person's total life in which energies are invested in both physical/intellectual activities and in positive emotional states." Sociologically, a central life interest is usually associated with a major role in life. And since central life interests can only emerge from positive emotional states, obsessive and compulsive activities can never qualify as such.

Dubin's (1992, pp. 41-42) examples clearly establish that either work (though not necessarily devotee work) or serious leisure can become a central life interest:

> A workaholic is an individual who literally lives and breathes an occupation or profession. Work hours know no limits, and off-work hours are usually filled with work-related concerns. Nothing pleases a workaholic more than to be working. Such an individual has a CLI [central life interest] in work.

A dedicated amateur or professional athlete will devote much more time and concentration to training than will be invested in actual competition. Over and over again athletes will practice their skills, hoping to bring themselves to a peak of performance. Even though practicing may be painful, the ultimate competitive edge produced by practice far outweighs in satisfaction and pride any aches and pains of preparation. Such people make their athletic life their CLI.

A committed gardener, stamp collector, opera buff, jet setter, cook, housewife, mountain climber, bird watcher, computer "hacker," novel reader, fisherman, or gambler (and you can add many more to the list from your own experiences) are all usually devoted to their activity as a central life interest. Give such individuals a chance to talk freely about themselves and they will quickly reveal their CLl through fixation on the subject and obvious emotional fervor with which they talk about it.

These are hobbyist and amateur activities. But career volunteers find a lively central life interest in their pursuits, too:

In American politics, and probably the politics of most Western countries, groups increasingly enter political life with a single issue as their rallying point. That single issue may be taxes, abortion, women's rights, the environment, consumerism, conservatism, or civil rights, and much activity and emotion is invested in "the movement." Adherents come to view themselves as personifying "good guys" who rally around a movement's single issue, making their movement their CLI.

As happens with leisure lifestyle, a leisure identity also arises in parallel with a person's leisure-based central life interest. In other words, a person's lifestyle in a given serious leisure activity gives expression to his central life interest there while forming the basis for a personal and community identity as some one who goes in for that activity.

Finally, we have seen that, to the extent that lifestyles form around complicated, absorbing, satisfying activities, they can also be viewed as behavioral expressions of the participants' central life interests (Dubin, 1992) in those activities. In the Information Age with its dwindling employment opportunities, most men and women will find more and more that the only kinds of central life interests open to them are the various amateur, hobbyist, and career volunteer activities composing serious leisure. Additionally, more and more of the underemployed will find themselves with a choice never before encountered in the history of work in the industrialized world: whether to make their, say, twenty-five-hour-a-week job their central life interest or turn to a serious leisure activity for this kind of attachment because the job is too insubstantial for an investment of positive emotional, physical, and intellectual energy. Of course, for the unemployed and the retired, serious leisure is their only recourse, if they are to have a central life interest at all. And there will always be a small number of people with sufficient time, energy, and opportunity to sustain more than one central life interest in either leisure or work, if not both.

In the future, jobless or relatively jobless as it is apt to be for many people, serious leisure will be the only remaining area in life where they can find an identity related to their distinctive personal qualities, qualities expressed in the course of realizing the rewards and benefits of serious leisure. Moreover, in the Information Age, it will be the only remaining area where these people can find a community role capable of fostering significant self-respect. When viewed through the prism of importance of work in Western society, most casual leisure activities, with their strong hedonic appeal of immediate intrinsic reward, are commonly dismissed as adding little to the self-respect of their participants.

Work and Leisure on Common Ground

Work and leisure have long been conceived of in Western civilization as distinctly separate spheres of life, a conception that appears to have reached its most extreme expression in the Protestant ethic. At least from that point in time to the present, the boundary demarcating both worlds has blurred somewhat, as evidenced in the histories presented in chapter 4. Nevertheless, as the Protestant ethic faded over the years and the work ethic moved in to replace it, we seemed to have gone out of our way to ensure that the boundary did not blur too much. Fixed work schedules have helped in this regard, as have our warm feelings about official time off: holidays, weekends, vacations from work (paid or not), and the like. Phrases such as "Thank God it's Friday" and "blue Monday" have also added their own special weight to this conception. And social scientists, for their part, have intellectualized the distinction by treating work and leisure as distinct social institutions.

This slant on the separateness of work and leisure is valid up to a point. Indeed, it would be difficult for most people to understand these two in any other way when, for them, the first is fundamentally uninteresting, if not unpleasant, obligation (the paycheck is nice, of course) and the second is happy refuge from it. More precisely, we can say, using the language of this book, that in both science and commonsense casual leisure is clearly distinguishable from work, be it work of the devotee or nondevotee variety.

But this book has also shown that not all work and leisure are so easily separated. While casual leisure and nondevotee work can be seen as separate coins, serious leisure and devotee work can only be logically seen as the two sides of a single third coin (see figure 7.1).

Figure 7.1
Work-leisure Coinage

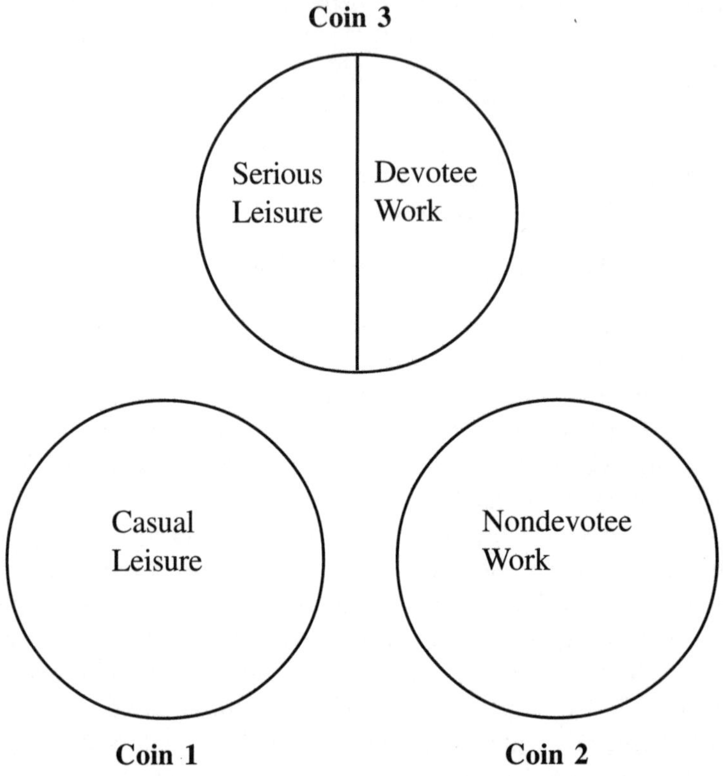

Coin 3

In other words it is evident here that the dominant popular and scientific conception of work and leisure as separate worlds is, and has been since at least the days of the Puritans, an unfortunate simplification of reality.

Unfortunate? Yes, because seeing work and leisure as separate entities has obscured the existence of the third coin, which portrays work and leisure as two highly fulfilling classes of activity that, except for the matter of remuneration, are much the same. It follows that many people, even if aware that some work can engender devotion to it, remain unaware of serious leisure as an alternative or additional area in which fulfilling activities can be found aplenty. This nescience prevents people from pursuing by way of such leisure the substantial cultural values and personal and social rewards that could be theirs. Moreover, this simplification places all of leisure in a bad moral light vis-à-vis work; leisure becomes the four-letter word, so to speak, not work. The prevailing work ethic has, as we have seen, painted all leisure in inferior tones. Pity therefore those unhappy retirees who saw their work as everything and now see their "forced" leisure as basically a badge of their own uselessness.

The third coin, minted as it has been with two seemingly incongruent sides, suggests that from primary school onward it is critical that the citizenry be educated about the nature and availability of fulfilling work and leisure in our time. Leisure education is a radical idea in North America, where the work ethic is still alive and well, but authorities there could nonetheless do no better than to emulate Israel. Such a program was recently established in its primary and secondary schools, using as its theoretical foundation the serious/ casual leisure perspective (Ruskin, 2000). Nowhere to my knowledge is there an educational program in place dealing with occupational devotion, but then the term is a neologism for an idea that received its first exposure in this book.

Conclusions

So occupational devotion seems destined to remain, even if it escapes the grasp of most workers. It is a cruel irony of every human economic system that many people wind up in places within it that fail to match their tastes, talents, and qualifications. This mismatch can be one of potential devotees working below their training and ability or working at this level but in a position that stifles fulfillment. And it happens, too, that people sometimes get mismatched in the opposite direction, by holding a job for which they are poorly qualified.

Serious leisure offers a refuge for those who are mismatched (as well as for many other people), in that, at least, they can still find a substantial pursuit to sink their teeth into. For leisure is more democratic than work; leisure choice is wider and not constrained by need to make a living according to the level on the economic situation scale to which a person aspires. And, who knows, having fallen in love with an amateur, hobbyist, or volunteer interest, whether some people might just not find their way, as some others before them have, into a parallel line of devotee work after all. For this to happen, however, they will have to become familiar with the work/leisure coinage metaphor. The outdated two-coin, separate world model serves us poorly, because it neglects the common ground.

Further, in tandem with this jostling for and carrying out of devotee work roles, social scientists should be expressing some of their own occupational devotion by systematically studying all aspects of the work/leisure common ground touched on in these pages. In this respect, given the scarcity of research on occupational devotees qua devotees, the most fruitful approach for the present is to examine them and their work using qualitative-exploratory methodology, with the intent of establishing a firm grounded theory of occupational devotion. Where we know little about the field being examined, it is prudent to explore it in open-ended fashion to ensure that all relevant processes and structures are identified and considered. Assuming this advice is acceptable at present, the time will eventually come when controlled, quantitative-confirmatory research will be needed to, for example, add precision to certain inductively generated propositions and to eliminate contradictions contained in rival hypotheses. There will also be, once a solid grounded theory is in place, a pressing need for survey research on the frequency of devotee occupations in various populations as well as on the demographic correlates of the devotees.

Be that as it may, researchers have been testing hypotheses for many years in the more established areas of the study of occupational devotion, most notably law and medicine (for a review see Macdonald, 1995, chap. 1). Still, they have not carried out their research from the perspective of occupational devotion, which is, among other things, a set of sensitizing concepts (Blumer, 1969) for systematically exploring this area. Nevertheless, it seems most probable that, for many years to come, research in the field will be both qualitative and quantitative as well as exploratory and confirmatory. This will occur, in part, because so many forms of devotee work remain to be explored and, in part, because many researchers in the sociology and psychology of work either are unfamiliar with exploratory procedures or are opposed to them on scientific grounds.

I hope it is clear in what has just been said that I am not indiscriminately championing qualitative-exploratory research over its counterpart, quantitative-confirmatory research. In my mind, it takes both to make a mature science. Exploration is, nevertheless, the most efficient and effective way to get to become familiar with an unknown area of social life, as occupational devotion presently is, by and large. But as I have indicated elsewhere (Stebbins, 2001b), exploration is a long process, consisting of a good number of concatenated, detailed studies that together lead to substantial and valid grounded theory. A single study of, say, theatre professionals, is but a decent start toward a grounded theory of that field of occupational devotion. It is a weaker start toward a theory of professional art and, as a start toward a theory of professionals in general or of all devotee work, it is weaker still.

So, inevitably, important scientific work remains to be done, once a reasonably solid grounded theory has been constructed. Some researchers at this advanced stage of knowledge will prefer to limit themselves to a priori hypothetical questions, while others, having an interest in a heretofore understudied area, will want to explore it and then set about examining certain hypotheses to emerge from that exploration. After this they may well report in the same write-up results from both phases. Either approach can bear fruit, providing the crucial personal and social elements of the devotee occupation under consideration are not inadvertently overlooked because the investigator is too narrowly focussed by theoretic framework or research design. In some areas of occupational devotion, mainly the public-centered professions studied in conjunction with their amateur counterparts, I believe we now know enough to avoid such oversights.

We have now come full circle. Kenyon Cox's advice set out in the epigraph is still apt and still worth following. Today and in the future, however, both aspiring and incumbent devotees will, if they are going to find and retain the kind of work they want, have to be more resourceful than in the past. But, then, for these talented and highly motivated souls, this may become just another interesting challenge that inspires their devotion.

References

Allison, M.T., & Duncan, M.C. (1988). Women, work, and flow. In M. Csikszentmihalyi & I.S. Csikszentmihalyi (Eds.), *Optimal experience: Psychological studies of flow in consciousness,* (pp. 118-137). New York: Cambridge University Press.

Apostle, R. (1992). Curling for cash: The "professionalization" of a popular Canadian sport. *Culture,* 12 (2), 17-28.

Applebaum, H. (1992). *The concept of work: Ancient, medieval, and modern.* Albany, NY: State University of New York Press.

Arai, S.M. (2000). A typology of volunteers for a changing sociopolitical context: The impact on social capital, citizenship, and civil society. *Loisir et Société/Society and Leisure,* 23, 327-352.

Arai, S.M., & Pedlar, A.M. (1997). Building Communities through leisure: Citizen participation in a healthy communities initiative. *Journal of Leisure Research,* 29, 167-182.

Aronowitz, S., & DiFazio, W. (1994). *The jobless future: Sci-tech and the dogma of work.* Minneapolis: University of Minnesota Press.

Atkinson, M. F. (2003). *Miscreants, malcontents, and mimesis: Sociogenic and psychogenic transformation in the Canadian tattoo figuration.* Toronto, ON: University of Toronto Press.

Baldwin, C.K., & Norris, P.A. (1999). Exploring the dimensions of serious leisure: Love me—love my dog. *Journal of Leisure Research,* 31, 1-17.

Barnes, H. E., (1965). *An intellectual and cultural history of the Western world* (3rd rev. ed.). New York: Dover Publications.

Barnes, J.A. (1954). Class and committees in a Norwegian island parish. *Human Relations,* 7, 39-58.

Barzun, J. (1956). *Music in American life.* Bloomington: Indiana University Press.

Beck, U. (2002). *The brave new world of work.* Cambridge, UK: Polity Press.

Becker, H.S. (1960). Notes on the concept of commitment. *American Journal of Sociology,* 66, 32-40.

Blendon, R.J., Deroches, C.M., Brodie, M., Benson, J.M., Rosen, A.B., Schneider, E., Altman, D.E., Zapert, K., Herrmann, M.J., & Steffenson, A.E. (2002). Patient safety views of practicing physicians and the public on medical errors. *New England Journal of Medicine,* 347 (12 December), 1033-1040.

Blumer, H. (1969). *Symbolic interactionism.* Englewood Cliffs, NJ: Prentice-Hall.

Borgatta, E.F. (1981). The small groups movement. *American Behavioral Scientist,* 24, 265-271.

Bott, E. (1957). *Family and social network.* London, UK: Tavistock Publications.

Bowen, C.D. (1935). *Friends and fiddlers.* Boston, MA: Little, Brown.

Braverman, H. (1974). *Labor and monopoly capital: The degradation of work in the twentieth century.* New York: Monthly Review Press.

Calgary Herald (2002). Masur leaves orchestra (15 July).

Calgary Herald (2003). Retired lifestyles not always golden, survey reveals. (Saturday, 1 March), p. D5.

Coakley, J. (2001). *Sport in society: Issues and controversies* (7th ed.). New York: McGraw-Hill.

Cohen, J. (2002). *Protestantism and capitalism: The mechanisms of influence*. New Yprk: Aldine de Gruyter.

Cross, G. (1990). *A social history of leisure since 1660*. State College, PA: Venture Publications.

Csikszentmihalyi, M. (1990). *Flow: The Psychology of Optimal Experience*. New York: Harper & Row.

Dubin, R. (1992). *Central life interests: Creative individualism in a complex world*. New Brunswick, NJ: Transaction Publishers.

Economist (2002). Too little money, too much paper (6 July).

Economist (2003a). A suitable case for treatment: medical-malpractice insurance (22 February).

Economist (2003b). Bernard Loiseau (8 March).

Erikson, K. T., (1966). *Wayward puritans*. New York: John Wiley.

Fassel, D. (2000). *Working ourselves to death: Costs of workaholism and the rewards of recovery*. Lincoln, NB: Universe.Com.

Fine, G.A. (1979). Small groups and culture creation: The idioculture of Little League baseball teams. *American Sociological Review*, 44, 733-745.

Fine, G.A., & Holyfield, L. (1996). Trusting fellows: Secrecy, trust, and voluntary allegiance in leisure spheres. *Social Psychological Quarterly*, 59, 22-38.

Florida, R. (2001). *The rise of the creative class and how it's transforming work, leisure, community and everyday life*. New York: Basic Books.

Floro, G.K. (1978). What to look for in a study of the volunteer in the work world. In R.P. Wolensky & E.J. Miller (Eds.), *The small city and regional community* (pp. 194-202). Stevens Point, WI: Foundation Press.

Fragnière, J.-P. (1987). Action sociale et bénévolat social. Rapport B-22. Berne, Switzerland: Conseil Suisse de la Science.

Freidson, E. (1990). Labors of love in theory and practice: A prospectus. In K. Erikson and S.P. Vallas (Eds.), *The nature of work: Sociological perspectives* (pp. 149-161). New Haven, CT: Yale University Press.

Gelber, S.M. (1999). *Hobbies: Leisure and the culture of work in America*. New York: Columbia University Press.

Gerth, Hans and Mills, C. Wright (Eds.) (1958). *From Max Weber: Essays in Sociology*. New York: Oxford University Press.

Gignac, T. (2003). Women in IT fight trend of gender bias. *Calgary Herald* (Saturday, 1 March), p. D1.

Gillespie, D.L., Leffler, A., & Lerner, E. (2002). If it weren't for my hobby, I'd have a life: Dog sports, serious leisure, and boundary negotiation. *Leisure Studies*, 21, 285-304.

Godbout, J. (1986). La participation: Instrument de professionalisation des loisirs. *Loisir et Société/Society and Leisure*, 9, 33-40.

Goff, S.J., Fick, D.S., & Oppliger, R.A. (1997). The moderating effect of spouse support on the relation between serious leisure and spouses' perceived leisure-family conflict. *Journal of Leisure Research*, 29, 47-60.

Goffman, E. (1961a). *Asylums: Essays on the social situation of mental patients and other inmates*. Garden City, NY: Doubleday.

Goffman, E. (1961b). *Encounters: Two studies in the sociology of interaction*. Indianapolis, IN: Bobbs-Merrill.

Habenstein, R.W. (1992). Sociology of occupations: The case of the American funeral director. In A.M. Rose (Ed.), *Human behavior and social processes* (pp. 225-246). Boston, MA: Houghton Mifflin.

Hall, R.H. (1986). *The dimensions of work.* Beverly Hills, CA: Sage.

Hamilton-Smith, E. (1993). In the Australian bush: Some reflections on serious leisure. *World Leisure & Recreation*, 35 (1), 10-13.

Hamilton-Smith, E. (1995). The connexions of scholarship. *Newsletter* (Official newsletter of RC13 of the International Sociological Association), March, 4-9.

Hastings, D.W., Kurth, S.B., Schloder, M., & Cyr, D. (1995). Reasons for participating in a serious leisure: Comparison of Canadian and U.S. masters swimmers. *International Review for Sociology of Sport,* 30, 101-119.

Haworth, J.T. (1986). Meaningful activity and psychological models of non-employment. *Leisure Studies*, 5, 281-297.

Haworth, J.T., & Hill, S. (1992). Work. leisure, and psychological well-being in a sample of young adults. *Journal of Community & Applied Social Psychology*, 2, 147-160.

Hewitt, J.P. (1991). *Self and society* (5th ed). Boston, MA: Allyn and Bacon.

Homans, G.C. (1974). *Social behavior*, rev. ed. New York: Harcourt, Brace, Jovanovich.

Howard, A. (Ed.). (1995). *The changing nature of work.* San Francisco, CA: Jossey-Bass.

Howe, C. (1995). Factors impacting leisure in middle-aged adults throughout the world: United States. *World Leisure & Recreation*, 37 (1), 37-38.

Huizinga, J. (1955). *Homo ludens: A study of the play element in culture.* Boston, MA: Beacon.

Jacobs, J.A. (2002). Detours on the road to equality: Women, work, and higher education. *Contexts: Understanding People in Their Social Worlds*, 2 (1), 32-41.

Johnson, G. (2002). Big step in the right direction. *Calgary Herald* (Friday, 26 July), p. F1.

Jones, J.F., & Herrick, J.M. (1976). *Citizens in service: Volunteers in social welfare during the Depression, 1929-1941.* East Lansing: Michigan State University Press.

Juniu, S., Tedrick, T., & Boyd, R. (1996). Leisure or work? Amateur and professional musicians' perception of rehearsal and performance. *Journal of Leisure Research*, 28, 44-56.

Kantor, R.M. (1968). Commitment and social organization. *American sociological review*, 33, 499-517.

Karp, D.A. (1989). The social construction of retirement among professionals. *Gerontologist*, 29, 750-760.

Kay, T. 1990. Active unemployment - A leisure pattern for the future. *Loisir et Société/Society and Leisure*, 12, 413-430.

Killinger, B. (1997). *Workaholism: The respectable addicts.* Toronto. ON: Firefly Books.

Lautenschlager, J. (1992). Le bénévolat: Une valeur traditionnelle au Canada. Ottawa, ON: Ministère du Multiculturalisme et Citoyenneté Canada, Gouvernement du Canada.

Lefkowitz, B. (1979). *Breaktime.* New York: Penguin.

Leicht, K.L., & Fennell, M.L. (2001). *Professional work: A sociological approach.* Malden, MA: Blackwell.

Lindesmith, A.R., Strauss, A.L., & Denzin, N.K. (1999). *Social psychology*, 8th ed. Thousand Oaks, CA: Sage.

Macdonald, K.M. (1995). *The sociology of the professions.* London, UK: Sage.

Machlowitz, M. (1980). *Workaholics: Living with them, working with them.* Reading, MA: Addison-Wesley.

Mackie, M. (1991). *Gender relations in Canada: Further explorations.* Toronto, ON: Butterworths.

Maffesoli, M. (1996). *The time of the tribes: The decline of individualism*, trans. by D. Smith. London, UK: Sage Publications.

Mannell, R.A. (1994). High investment activity and life satisfaction among older adults: Committed serious leisure and flow activities. In J.R. Kelly (Ed.), *Activity and aging: Staying involved in later life* (pp. 125-145). Newbury Park, CA: Sage.

Marshall, T.H. (1963). *Sociology at the crossroads and other essays.* London, UK: Heinemann.

McQuarrie, F., & Jackson, E.L. (1996). Connections between negotiation of leisure constraints and serious leisure: An exploratory study of adult amateur ice skaters. *Loisir et Société/Society and Leisure*, 19, 459-483.

Montanera, D. (2003). Designing woman closes shop. *Calgary Herald*, Sunday 2 February, p. D12.

Nahrstedt, W. (2000). Global edutainment: The role of leisure education for community development. In A. Sivan & H. Ruskin (Eds.), *Leisure education, community development and populations with special needs* (pp. 65-74). London, UK: CAB International.

Nicols, G., & King. L. (1999). Redefining the recruitment niche for the Guide Association in the United Kingdom. *Leisure Sciences*, 21, 307-320.

Olmsted, A.D. (1991). Collecting: Leisure, investment, or obsession? *Journal of Social Behavior and Personality*, 6, 287-306.

Parker, S.R. (1996). Serious leisure - A middle-class phenomenon? In M. Collins (Ed.), *Leisure in industrial and post-industrial societies* (pp. 327-332). Eastbourne, UK: Leisure Studies Association.

Paterson, A. (1983). Becoming a judge. In R. Dingwall & P. Lewis (Eds), *The sociology of professions: Lawyers, doctors, and others* (pp. 263-87). London, UK: The Macmillan Press.

Phillips, Bernard (2001). *Beyond sociology's tower of Babel: Reconstructing the scientific method.* Hawthorne, NY: Aldine de Gruyter.

Riesman, D. (1952). *Faces in the crowd: Individual studies in character and politics.* New Haven, CT: Yale University Press.

Riesman, D. (1961). *The lonely crowd: A study of the changing American character* (rev. ed.). New Haven, CT: Yale University Press.

Rifkin, J. (1995). *The end of work: The decline of the global labor force and the dawn of the post-market era.* New York: G.P. Putnam's Sons.

Rinehart, J.W. (1996). *The tyranny of work: Alienation and the labour process* (3rd ed.). Toronto, ON: Harcourt Brace Canada.

Ritzer, G., & Walczak, D. (1986). *Working: Conflict and change* (3rd ed). Englewood Cliffs, NJ: Prentice-Hall.

Robinson, J.P., & Godbey G. (1997). *Time for life: The surprising ways Americans use their time.* University Park: Pennsylvania State University Press.

Rocher, G. (1972). *A general introduction to sociology: A theoretical perspective*, trans, by P. Sheriff. Toronto, ON: Macmillan Co. of Canada.

Ruskin, H. (2002). Implementation of serious leisure as part of leisure education in Israel. *European leisure and recreation* (ELRA Newsletter) (April), pp. 1-3.

Samuel, N. (1994). The future of leisure time. In *New Routes for Leisure* (pp. 45-57). Lisbon, Portugal: Instituto de Ciências Sociais, Universidade de Lisboa.

Schor, J.B. (1991). *The overworked American: The unexpected decline of leisure.* New York: Basic Books.

Schumacher, E.F. (1980). *Good work.* New York: Harper Colophon Books.

Siegenthaler, K.L., & Gonsalez, G.L. (1997). Youth sports as serious leisure: A critique. *Journal of Sport and Social Issues*, 21, 298-314.

Siegenthaler, K.L., & Lam, T.C.M. (1992). Commitment and ego-involvement in recreational tennis. *Leisure Studies*, 14, 303-315.

Silver, M.L. (1982). The structure of craft work: The construction industry. In P.L. Stewart and M.G. Cantor (Eds.), *Varieties of work* (pp. 235-252). Beverly Hills, CA: Sage.

Slater, P.E. (1970). *The pursuit of loneliness: American culture at the breaking point.* Boston, MA: Beacon.

Slobodian, L. (2003). Crash expert takes his road show overseas. *The Calgary Herald,* Sunday, 1 June.

Smith, P., Kendall, L., & Hullin, C. (1969). *The measurement of satisfaction in work and retirement.* Chicago, IL: Rand McNally.

Sonnenberg, R. (1996). *Living with workaholism.* St. Louis, MO: Concordia Publishing House.

Statistics Canada (2001). Caring Canadians, involved Canadians: Highlights from the 2000 national survey of giving, volunteering, and participating (cat. No. 71-542-XIE). Ottawa, ON: Ministry of Industry, Government of Canada.

Stebbins, R.A. (1970a). Career: The subjective approach. *Sociological Quarterly,* 11, 32-49.

Stebbins, R.A. (1970b). On misunderstanding the concept of commitment: A theoretical clarification. *Social Forces,* 48 (4), 526-529.

Stebbins, R.A. (1979). *Amateurs: On the margin between work and leisure.* Beverly Hills, CA: Sage.

Stebbins, R.A. (1981). Toward a social psychology of stage fright. In M. Hart & S. Birrell (Eds.), *Sport in the sociocultural process* (pp. 156-163). Dubuque, IA: W.C. Brown.

Stebbins, R.A. (1982). Serious leisure: a conceptual statement. *Pacific Sociological Review,* 25, 251-272.

Stebbins, R.A. (1992). *Amateurs, professionals, and serious leisure.* Montreal, QC and Kingston, ON: McGill-Queen's University Press.

Stebbins, R.A. (1993). *Canadian football: The view from the helmet.* Toronto: Canadian Scholars Press

Stebbins, R.A. (1994). The liberal arts hobbies: A neglected subtype of serious leisure. *Loisir et Société/Society and Leisure,* 16, 173-186.

Stebbins, R.A. (1996a). *The barbershop singer: Inside the social world of a musical hobby.* Toronto, ON: University of Toronto Press.

Stebbins, R.A. (1996b). Volunteering: A serious leisure perspective. *Nonprofit and Voluntary Action Quarterly,* 25, 211-224.

Stebbins, R.A. (1997a). Casual leisure: A conceptual statement. *Leisure Studies,* 16, 17-25.

Stebbins, R.A. (1997b). Lifestyle as a generic concept in ethnographic research. *Quality & Quantity,* 31, 347-360.

Stebbins, R.A. (1998). *The urban francophone volunteer: Searching for personal meaning and community growth in a linguistic minority,* Vol. 3, No. 2 (New Scholars-New Visions in Canadian Studies quarterly monographs series). Seattle: University of Washington, Canadian Studies Centre.

Stebbins, R.A. (1999). Encouraging youthful involvement in the arts: A serious leisure framework. *Lo Spettacolo,* 49 (July-September), 261-275.

Stebbins, R.A. (2000a). The extraprofessional life: Leisure, retirement, and unemployment. *Current Sociology,* 48, 1-27.

Stebbins, R.A. (2000b). Optimal leisure lifestyle: Combining serious and casual leisure for personal well-being. In M.C. Cabeza (Ed.), *Leisure and human development: Proposals for the 6th World Leisure Congress* (pp. 101-107). Bilbao, Spain: University of Deusto (2000).

Stebbins, R.A. (2001a). *New directions in the theory and research of serious leisure,* Mellen Studies in Sociology, vol. 28. Lewiston, NY: Edwin Mellen.

Stebbins, R.A. (2001b). *Exploratory research in the social sciences,* Sage University Paper Series on Qualitative Research Methods, vol. 48. Thousand Oaks, CA: Sage Publications.

Stebbins,R.A. (2001c). The costs and benefits of hedonism: Some consequences of taking casual leisure seriously. *Leisure Studies*, 20, 305-309.

Stebbins, R.A. (2001d). Volunteering—mainstream and marginal: Preserving the leisure experience. In M. Graham and M. Foley (Eds.), *Volunteering in leisure: Marginal or inclusive?* (LSA Publication No. 75) (pp. 1-10). Eastbourne, UK: Leisure Studies Association.

Stebbins, R.A. (2002a). *The Organizational Basis of Leisure Participation: A Motivational Exploration.* State College, PA: Venture Publishing.

Stebbins, R.A. (2002b). Choice in experiential definitions of leisure. *Leisure Studies Association Newsletter*, 63 (November), 18-20.

Stebbins, R.A. (in press). Stamp collecting. In G.S. Cross (Ed.), *Encyclopedia of recreation and leisure in America.* New York: Charles Scribners' Sons.

Stone, G.P. (1971). American sports: Play and display. In E. Dunning (Ed.), *The sociology of sport: A selection of readings* (pp. 47-65). Toronto, ON: University of Toronto Press.

Terkel, S. (1972). *Working.* New York: Random House.

Tinder, G. (1975). *Tolerance: Toward a new civility.* Amherst: University of Massachusetts Press.

Towers Perrin (2003). Working today: Exploring employees' emotional connection to their jobs. New York.

U.S. Census Bureau (2000). *Statistical Abstract of the United States: 2000.* Washington, DC: Government of the United States.

U.S. Department of Labor Employment and Training Administration (1991). *Dictionary of occupational titles*, Vol. 1 (4th ed., revised). Lanham, MD: Bernan Press.

Unruh, D.R. (1979). Characteristics and types of participation in social worlds. *Symbolic Interaction*, 2, 115-130.

Unruh, D.R. (1980). The nature of social worlds. *Pacific Sociological Review*, 23, 271-296.

Van Til, J. (1988). *Mapping the third sector: Voluntarism in a changing political economy.* New York: The Foundation Center.

Veal, A.J. (1993). The concept of lifestyle: A review. *Leisure Studies*, 12, 233-252.

Wallace, J.E. (1995a). Corporatist control and organizational commitment among professionals: The case of lawyers working in law firms. *Social Forces*, 73, 811-839.

Wallace, J.E. (1995b). Organizational and professional commitment in professional and nonprofessional organizations. *Administrative Science quarterly*, 40, 228-255.

Whannel, G. (1983). *Blowing the whistle: The politics of sport.* London, UK: Pluto Press.

Whyte, W.H., Jr. (1956). *The organization man.* Gardern City, NY: Doubleday.

Williams, R.M., Jr. (2000). American society. In E.F. Borgatta & R.J.V. Montgomery (Eds.), *Encyclopedia of sociology*, 2nd ed., Vol. 1 (pp. 140-148). New York: Macmillan.

Yair, G. (1990). The commitment to long-distance running and level of activities. *Journal of Leisure Research*, 22, 213-227.

Yankelovich, D. (1981). *New rules: Searching for self-fulfillment in a world turned upside down.* New York: Random House.

Yoder, D.G. (1997). A model for commodity intensive serious leisure. *Journal of Leisure Research*, 29, 407-429.

Zuzanek, J. (1996). Canada. In G. Cushman, A.J. Veal, & J. Zuzanek (Eds.), *World leisure participation: Free time in the global village* (pp. 35-76). Wallingford, Oxon, UK: CAB International.

Index

Addiction to work, 22, 28
Advisors, 12
Alienation, 111-112. *See also* Work, deskilling of
Allison, M.T., 7
Altman, D.E., 84
Amateurism, history of, 55-57
Amateurs, 50-51
  become professionals, 73-74
  compared with dabblers (players, dilettantes), 56, 57
  definitions of, 51, 57
  preprofessional, 74, 88, 90
  See also Amateurism, history of; Serious leisure
Apostle, R., 51
Applebaum, H., 28, 31
Arai, S.M., 55, 63
Aronowitz, S., 31, 62, 111-112, 114
Atkinson, M.F., 40

Baldwin, C.K., 15, 70
Barnes, H.E., 35
Barnes, J.A., 81
Barzun, J., 56
Beck, B., 31, 33
Becker, H.S., 18, 63
Benson, J.M., 84
Birrell, S., 129
Blendon, R.J., 84
Blumer, H., 122
Boredom, 9, 10, 19, 88-89
Borgatta, E.F., 68, 130
Bott, E., 81
Boyd, R., 76
Bowen, C.D., 100
Braverman, H., 28
Brodie, M., 84
Bunyan, J., 34
Bureaucracy, 3, 9, 54
  and alienation, 111-112

  and leisure career, 70
  and occupational devotion, 3, 9, 54, 82-84
  and remuneration, 96-97

Cabeza, M.C., 129
Cantor, M.G., 128
Capitalism, 23-24, 25, 26, 35, 57-58
Career, 70-71
  continuity in, 70-71
  definition of leisure, 70
  in devotee work, 86-89
  in serious leisure, 49-50, 52-53, 64, 67, 69-71
  stages of, 87
  in work (general), 10
Casual leisure, 41-42, 50, 107, 119
  benefits of, 104
  creativity in, 104
  definition of, 50
  "edutainment" in, 104
  and interpersonal relationships, 104
  regeneration (re-creation) in, 104
  and selfishness, 101-103
  and self-gratification, 53
  types of, 50
  uncontrollability of, 101
  and well-being, 104
Central life interest, 117-119
  definition of, 117
Civil labor, 31
Client-centered professions and professionals, 3, 11, 74, 93. *See also* Professions and professionals
Coakley, J., 99
Cohen, J., 24
Collins, M., 128
Commitment, 17-18
  continuance, 18
  value, 17-18
Conspicuous consumption, 22, 26

131